Lipton®

MAKE IT

MICROWAVE

PUBLICATIONS
INTERNATIONAL, LTD.

Lipton, Flo-Thru and Wish-Bone are registered trademarks of Thomas J. Lipton, Inc., Englewood Cliffs, New Jersey 07632.

Knox is a registered trademark of Knox Gelatine, Inc., Englewood Cliffs, New Jersey 07632.

Lawry's is a registered trademark of Lawry's Foods, Inc., Los Angeles, California 90065.

Imperial is a registered trademark of Lever Brothers, New York, New York 10022.

Equal is a registered trademark of The NutraSweet Co., Chicago, Illinois 60680.

Project Director: Anna Marie Coccia—Manager, Lipton Test Kitchens.

The Lipton Microwave Center:

Lipton Recipe Development—Alyssa A. Alia and The Lipton Kitchens Staff: Ronda DiGuglielmo, Senior Home Economist; Marla Edelstein, Senior Home Economist; Cristina Bouman, Home Economist.

Lawry's Recipe Development—The Lawry's Consumer Kitchens Staff: Robin Ruschman, Consumer Kitchens Manager; Cindy Cutler, Home Economist; Maribeth Drogosz, Home Economist.

Food Styling: Alyssa A. Alia
Kitchen Associate: Wendy Walters
Photographer: Daniel J. Piszczatoski
Photography Assistant: Keith Thomas
Prop Stylist: Stacey Smith

ACKNOWLEDGMENT
Thomas J. Lipton, Inc. wishes to acknowledge Sasaki for a variety of flatware, glassware and dinnerware used in many of the photos in this cookbook.

This edition published by:
Publications International, Ltd.
7373 N. Cicero Avenue
Lincolnwood, Illinois 60646

Library of Congress Catalog Card Number: 89-69866

ISBN: 0-88176-909-6

Pictured on the front cover (*clockwise from right*): Chunky Chicken Noodle Soup with Vegetables (*see page 56*), Simply Green Beans (*see page 27*), Springtime Noodles Alfredo (*see page 24*), Marinated Shrimp Italiano (*see page 72*) and Chocolate-Pecan & Caramel Pie (*see page 78*).

Pictured on the back cover: Souper Nachos (*see page 4*), Homestyle Zucchini and Tomatoes (*see page 32*), Oriental Vegetable Stir-Fry (*see page 28*) and Pink Tea Rose, Lipton Iced Tea (*see page 90*) and Fruit 'n Spice Margarita (*see page 88*).

Printed and bound in Yugoslavia. ®

h g f e d c b a

Lipton

MAKE IT MICROWAVE

MICROWAVE DIRECTIONS

Numerous variables, such as the microwave oven's rated wattage and the starting temperature, shape, amount and depth of the food, can affect cooking time; therefore, microwave cooking times in this cookbook are approximate. Use the cooking times as a guideline and check doneness before adding more time. Lower wattage ovens may consistently require longer cooking times.

APPETIZERS

SOUPER NACHOS

¼ pound ground beef
2 envelopes Lipton Tomato Cup-
   a-Soup Instant Soup
½ cup water
1 teaspoon red wine vinegar
½ to 1 teaspoon chili powder

Tortilla chips (about 30)
¼ cup chopped green onions
   (optional)
1 cup shredded Monterey Jack
   or Cheddar cheese (about
   3 ounces)

In small microwave-safe bowl, microwave ground beef at HIGH (Full Power) 2 minutes or until no longer pink; drain. Stir in instant tomato soup mix, water, vinegar and chili powder. Microwave at HIGH 1½ minutes or until thickened, stirring once. Arrange ½ of the tortilla chips in one layer on microwave-safe plate, then top with ½ of the ground beef mixture, onions and cheese; repeat layer. Microwave at HIGH 1½ minutes or until cheese is melted.

Makes 4 snack-size or 1 main-dish serving

CONVENTIONAL DIRECTIONS: Preheat oven to 375°. In small skillet, brown ground beef; drain. Stir in instant tomato soup mix, water, vinegar and chili powder. Cook, stirring frequently, 1 minute or until mixture thickens. Arrange as above on ovenproof plate or baking dish. Bake 10 minutes or until cheese is melted.

Making Plain Croutons
In microwave-safe shallow baking dish, place 2 cups (½ inch) bread cubes.
Microwave at High (Full Power) 3 to 4 minutes, stirring once.

◆◆◆

FETTUCCINE ALFREDO WITH SHIITAKE MUSHROOMS

1 tablespoon olive or vegetable
   oil
2 medium cloves garlic, finely
   chopped
1 cup sliced shiitake or white
   mushrooms
2 tablespoons dry white wine
1 tablespoon finely chopped
   fresh basil leaves*

1½ cups milk
1 cup canned crushed tomatoes
½ cup water
1 package Lipton Noodles &
   Sauce - Alfredo
Dash pepper

In 1½-quart microwave-safe casserole, microwave oil with garlic, uncovered, at HIGH (Full Power) 1 minute. Add mushrooms, wine and basil and microwave 1½ minutes or until mushrooms are tender. Stir in remaining ingredients and microwave at HIGH 13 to 14 minutes or until noodles are tender. Let stand 5 minutes. Garnish, if desired, with additional basil leaves and cherry tomatoes.

Makes about 4 appetizer or 2 main-dish servings

*Substitution: Use ½ teaspoon dried basil leaves.

CONVENTIONAL DIRECTIONS: Add 2 tablespoons Imperial Margarine. In medium skillet, heat oil and cook garlic over medium heat 30 seconds. Add mushrooms, wine and basil and cook over medium heat, stirring occasionally, 2 minutes or until mushrooms are tender. Stir in remaining ingredients plus margarine. Bring to the boiling point, then continue boiling, stirring occasionally, 8 minutes or until noodles are tender.

CHILI DOG BITES

1 envelope Lipton Tomato Cup-
   a-Soup Instant Soup
⅓ cup water
⅛ teaspoon chili powder

3 frankfurters, cut into 6 pieces
18 cubes (1½ inches each)
   American or Cheddar
   cheese (about 4 ounces)

In shallow 1-quart microwave-safe casserole, blend instant tomato soup mix, water and chili powder. Add frankfurters in one layer, turning to coat; cover with wax paper. Microwave at HIGH (Full Power) 1½ minutes or until heated through. Onto toothpicks, thread one frankfurter slice and one cheese cube. Place frankfurter-side down in casserole and microwave at HIGH 30 seconds or until cheese melts slightly.

Makes 18 appetizers

CONVENTIONAL DIRECTIONS: In medium skillet, blend instant tomato soup mix, water and chili powder. Add frankfurters and cook over medium heat, stirring frequently, 2 minutes or until thickened. Onto toothpicks, thread frankfurters as above. Place frankfurter-side down in skillet and cook over low heat 2 minutes or until cheese melts slightly.

Fettuccine Alfredo with Shiitake Mushrooms

STUFFED QUESADILLAS

5 tablespoons Wish-Bone Italian Dressing
1 large onion, finely chopped
1 large tomato, finely chopped
½ teaspoon chili powder

2 tablespoons finely chopped fresh coriander (cilantro)
6 flour tortillas
2 cups shredded Monterey Jack cheese (about 6 ounces)

In 2-quart casserole, microwave 3 tablespoons Italian dressing, onion, tomato and chili powder, uncovered, at HIGH (Full Power) 10 minutes or until onion is tender and mixture is thickened; stir in coriander.

On paper towels, microwave tortillas at HIGH 30 seconds to soften. On ½ of each tortilla, sprinkle ⅓ cup cheese and top with 2 tablespoons onion mixture; fold tortilla over to cover filling. Brush tortillas with remaining 2 tablespoons Italian dressing. On wax-paper-lined plate, place 3 filled tortillas. Microwave at HIGH 45 seconds or until cheese is melted; repeat with remaining tortillas.

Makes about 6 appetizer servings

CONVENTIONAL DIRECTIONS: Preheat oven to 400°. In medium skillet, heat 3 tablespoons Italian dressing and cook onion over medium-high heat, stirring occasionally, 3 minutes or until almost tender. Stir in tomato and chili powder and cook 3 minutes or until mixture is thickened; stir in coriander. On baking pan, bake tortillas 3 minutes or until softened. Prepare tortillas as above. On greased baking pan, bake tortillas 5 minutes or until cheese is melted.

● Also terrific with Wish-Bone Blended Italian or Herbal Italian Dressing.

CHICKEN WINGS WITH HONEY & ORANGE SAUCE

12 chicken wings (about 2 pounds)
1 envelope Lipton Golden Onion Recipe Soup Mix
⅓ cup honey
¼ cup water
¼ cup frozen concentrated orange juice, partially thawed and undiluted

¼ cup sherry
1 tablespoon prepared mustard
2 teaspoons soy sauce
¼ teaspoon ground ginger
3 dashes hot pepper sauce

Cut tips off chicken wings (save tips for soup). Cut chicken wings in half at joint.

In 13×9-inch microwave-safe baking dish, blend remaining ingredients; add chicken and turn to coat. Microwave uncovered at HIGH (Full Power), basting and rearranging chicken occasionally, 20 minutes or until chicken is done and sauce is thickened. Let stand uncovered 5 minutes.

Makes 24 appetizers

CONVENTIONAL DIRECTIONS: Preheat oven to 350°. In 13×9-inch baking dish, prepare chicken wings and sauce as above. Bake uncovered, basting occasionally, 40 minutes or until chicken is done and sauce is thickened.

WARM SPINACH SALAD

1 quart fresh spinach leaves,
    torn into pieces
1 cup sliced mushrooms
½ cup shredded carrots

4 slices bacon
⅓ cup Wish-Bone Italian
    Dressing
¼ teaspoon dry mustard

In medium bowl, toss spinach, mushrooms and carrots; set aside.

In 9- or 10-inch microwave-safe pie plate, arrange bacon; cover with paper towel. Microwave at HIGH (Full Power) 3½ minutes or until crisp; drain and crumble. Into pie plate, add Italian dressing blended with mustard and microwave at HIGH 1 minute or until heated through. Pour over spinach mixture; add bacon and toss.

Makes about 4 appetizer servings

CONVENTIONAL DIRECTIONS: In medium bowl, toss spinach as above. In small skillet, cook bacon until crisp; drain and crumble. Into skillet, add Italian dressing blended with mustard; heat through. Pour over spinach mixture; add bacon and toss.

● Also terrific with Wish-Bone Robusto Italian, Blended Italian, Italian & Cheese, Lite Italian, Herbal Italian, Olive Oil Vinaigrette or Classic Dijon Vinaigrette Dressing.

APPETIZER MEATBALLS ITALIANO

1 package (1.5 ounces) Lawry's
    Spaghetti Sauce Seasoning
    Blend with Imported
    Mushrooms
1 can (6 ounces) tomato paste
1¾ cups water
½ cup dry red wine
2 tablespoons Imperial
    Margarine or vegetable oil

1 pound ground beef
1 egg, slightly beaten
½ cup plain dry bread crumbs
¼ cup finely chopped green
    pepper
1 teaspoon Lawry's Seasoned
    Salt
¼ teaspoon Lawry's Seasoned
    Pepper

In 1-quart glass measure, blend spaghetti sauce seasoning blend with imported mushrooms, tomato paste, water, wine and margarine. Cover with wax paper and microwave at HIGH (Full Power) 15 minutes, stirring every 4 minutes. Reserve ¼ cup sauce. In medium bowl, thoroughly combine ground beef, egg, bread crumbs, green pepper, seasoned salt, seasoned pepper and ¼ cup reserved sauce. Shape into 1-inch meatballs. Arrange in a circle on 10-inch microwave-safe pie plate. Cover with wax paper and microwave at HIGH 5 minutes, turning dish once after 2½ minutes. Drain on paper towels, then add to remaining sauce.

Makes 45 meatballs

CONVENTIONAL DIRECTIONS: In medium saucepan, blend spaghetti sauce seasoning blend with imported mushrooms, tomato paste, water, wine and margarine. Bring to a boil, then simmer uncovered 25 minutes, stirring occasionally. Reserve ¼ cup sauce. In medium bowl, thoroughly combine ground beef, egg, bread crumbs, green pepper, seasoned salt, seasoned pepper and reserved ¼ cup sauce. Shape into 1-inch meatballs. In large skillet, brown meatballs and cook over medium heat 10 minutes. Drain on paper towels, then add to remaining sauce.

MARIACHI DRUMSTICKS

1¼ cups crushed plain tortilla
    chips
1 package (1.25 ounces) Lawry's
    Taco Seasoning Mix

18 to 20 chicken drummettes
Salsa

In large plastic bag, combine tortilla chips with taco seasoning mix. Dampen chicken with water and shake off excess. Place a few pieces at a time in plastic bag; shake thoroughly to coat with chips. Arrange chicken on greased microwave-safe pie plate in "spoke" pattern with thick ends of chicken toward outside edge of plate. Cover with wax paper. Microwave at MEDIUM-HIGH (70% Power) 8 to 10 minutes or until chicken is crispy, turning plate after 5 minutes. Serve with salsa for dipping. *Makes about 20 drummettes*

CONVENTIONAL DIRECTIONS: Preheat oven to 350°. Prepare and coat chicken as above. Arrange on greased shallow baking pan; bake uncovered 30 minutes or until chicken is crispy. Serve as above.

POTATO WRAPS

4 small new potatoes (1½ inch
    diameter each)
½ teaspoon Lawry's Seasoned
    Salt
½ teaspoon Lawry's Seasoned
    Pepper

¼ teaspoon crushed bay leaves
8 slices bacon, cut in half
    crosswise

Wash potatoes and cut into quarters. Sprinkle each with a mixture of seasoned salt, seasoned pepper and bay leaves. Wrap 1 bacon piece around each potato piece. Sprinkle with any remaining seasonings. Place two sheets of paper towel in round microwave-safe pie plate. Arrange potato pieces on plate. Microwave at HIGH (Full Power) 7 to 8 minutes or until bacon is crispy and potatoes are cooked through, turning dish after 5 minutes. Let stand on paper towels 1 minute. Serve, if desired, with sour cream and chives. *Makes 16 appetizers*

CONVENTIONAL DIRECTIONS: Preheat oven to 400°. Prepare potatoes as above. Place in baking dish and bake uncovered 20 minutes or until bacon is crispy and potatoes are cooked through. Drain on paper towels.

Mariachi Drumsticks (top) and Potato Wraps (bottom)

STEAMED MUSSELS IN WHITE WINE

⅓ cup Wish-Bone Italian
   Dressing
½ cup chopped shallots or
   onions
⅓ cup dry white wine
½ cup chopped parsley

¼ cup water
   Generous dash crushed red
   pepper
3 pounds mussels, well
   scrubbed

In 3-quart microwave-safe casserole, microwave Italian dressing with shallots, uncovered, at HIGH (Full Power) 2 minutes or until tender. Add wine, parsley, water and red pepper. Microwave covered at HIGH 1½ minutes or until boiling. Add mussels and microwave covered at HIGH 5 minutes or until shells open, stirring once. (Discard any unopened shells.) Let stand covered 3 minutes. Serve, if desired, with Italian or French bread.

Makes about 6 appetizer or 3 main-dish servings

CONVENTIONAL DIRECTIONS: Increase wine to ⅔ cup. In large saucepan or stockpot, heat Italian dressing and cook shallots over medium heat, stirring occasionally, 2 minutes or until tender. Add remaining ingredients. Bring to a boil, then simmer covered 4 minutes or until shells open. (Discard any unopened shells.) Serve as above.

● Also terrific with Wish-Bone Robusto Italian, Blended Italian or Olive Oil Vinaigrette Dressing.

NOODLES WITH CILANTRO PESTO

⅔ cup loosely packed fresh
   cilantro (coriander)
⅔ cup loosely packed parsley
3 tablespoons olive oil
1 tablespoon pignoli (pine) nuts
1 medium clove garlic
2 tablespoons grated Parmesan
   cheese

1½ cups water
½ cup milk
2 tablespoons Imperial
   Margarine
1 package Lipton Noodles &
   Sauce - Alfredo

In blender or food processor, process cilantro, parsley, oil, nuts and garlic until smooth. Stir in cheese; set aside.

In 1½-quart microwave-safe casserole, combine water, milk, margarine and noodles & Alfredo sauce. Microwave uncovered at HIGH (Full Power) 13 to 14 minutes or until noodles are tender; stir. Serve pesto over hot noodles and garnish, if desired, with additional pignoli nuts. Serve, if desired, with grilled chicken. *Makes 4 appetizer or 2 main-dish servings*

CONVENTIONAL DIRECTIONS: Prepare pesto as above. In medium saucepan, bring water, milk and margarine to the boiling point. Stir in noodles & Alfredo sauce and continue boiling over medium heat, stirring occasionally, 8 minutes or until noodles are tender. Serve as above.

Steamed Mussels in White Wine

WARM MUSHROOM & BACON DIP

6 slices bacon
½ pound mushrooms, thinly
  sliced
2 medium cloves garlic, finely
  chopped
1 envelope Lipton Golden Onion
  or Onion Recipe Soup Mix

⅛ teaspoon pepper
1 package (8 ounces) cream
  cheese, softened
1 container (8 ounces) sour
  cream
Assorted crackers or sliced
  breads

In 2-quart microwave-safe casserole, arrange bacon; cover with paper towel. Microwave at HIGH (Full Power) 5 minutes or until crisp; remove bacon and crumble. Reserve 2½ tablespoons drippings. Add mushrooms and garlic to reserved drippings and microwave uncovered at HIGH 2 minutes or until mushrooms are tender, stirring once. Add golden onion recipe soup mix and pepper, then cream cheese; combine thoroughly.

Microwave uncovered at MEDIUM (50% Power), stirring frequently, 3 minutes or until cream cheese is melted. Stir in sour cream and bacon. Microwave uncovered at MEDIUM 3 minutes or until heated through, stirring once. Garnish, if desired, with parsley and additional mushrooms and bacon. Serve with crackers.

Makes about 2 cups dip

CONVENTIONAL DIRECTIONS: In medium skillet, cook bacon; remove and crumble. Reserve 2½ tablespoons drippings. Add mushrooms and garlic to reserved drippings and cook over medium heat, stirring occasionally, 5 minutes or until mushrooms are tender and liquid is almost evaporated. Add golden onion recipe soup mix and pepper, then cream cheese; combine thoroughly. Simmer, stirring constantly, until cream cheese is melted. Stir in sour cream and bacon; heat through. Garnish and serve as above.

Cooking Bacon

On microwave-safe rack or paper-towel-lined plate, arrange bacon; cover with paper towel. Microwave at HIGH (Full Power):

2 slices – 1½ to 2 minutes
4 slices – 2½ to 3½ minutes
6 slices – 4 to 5 minutes
8 slices – 6½ to 7½ minutes

◆◆◆

CREAMY ZUCCHINI AND ONION SPREAD

¼ cup Imperial Margarine
2 medium zucchini, sliced
1 medium onion, sliced
1 envelope Knox Unflavored
    Gelatine
¼ cup cold water
1 cup (½ pint) whipping or
    heavy cream

½ cup sour cream
⅓ cup grated Parmesan cheese
1 tablespoon snipped fresh dill*
1 teaspoon salt
Dash red pepper
Assorted breads and crackers

In 2-quart microwave-safe casserole, microwave margarine, zucchini and onion, loosely covered with wax paper, at HIGH (Full Power) 7 minutes or until vegetables are very tender, stirring twice. Remove wax paper and let stand 10 minutes.

In 1-cup glass measure, sprinkle unflavored gelatine over cold water; let stand 2 minutes. Microwave at HIGH 40 seconds. Stir thoroughly, then let stand 2 minutes or until gelatine is completely dissolved.

In blender or food processor, process cream, sour cream, cheese, dill, salt and pepper until smooth. Add zucchini mixture and lukewarm gelatine mixture; process until smooth, about 30 seconds. Pour into 8×4×3-inch loaf pan; chill until firm, about 3 hours. Unmold and serve with breads.

Makes about 3 cups spread

*Substitution: Use 2 teaspoons dried dill weed.

CONVENTIONAL DIRECTIONS: Increase sour cream to ¾ cup. In medium skillet, melt margarine and cook zucchini with onion over medium heat, stirring occasionally, 10 minutes or until very tender; let cool. In small saucepan, sprinkle unflavored gelatine over cold water; let stand 1 minute. Stir over low heat until gelatine is completely dissolved, about 3 minutes. Remove from heat and let stand until lukewarm, about 2 minutes. Proceed as above.

MEATBALL NIBBLES

1 pound ground beef
2 envelopes Lipton Onion Cup-
    a-Soup Instant Soup
1 egg

⅓ cup plain dry bread crumbs
¼ cup ketchup
2 tablespoons finely chopped
    parsley

In medium bowl, combine all ingredients. Shape into 1-inch meatballs; divide into three batches. Place one batch on 9-inch microwave-safe round shallow dish; cover with wax paper. Microwave at HIGH (Full Power) 4 minutes or until done. Repeat with remaining batches. Serve, if desired, with assorted mustards or tomato sauce.

Makes about 4 dozen meatballs

CONVENTIONAL DIRECTIONS: Preheat oven to 375°. Shape meatballs as above. In shallow baking pan, arrange meatballs and bake 18 minutes or until done. Serve as above.

Top: Creamy Zucchini and Onion Spread
Bottom: Roasted Red Pepper Mousse Spread (see page 20)

ROASTED RED PEPPER MOUSSE SPREAD

1 envelope Knox Unflavored
    Gelatine
⅓ cup cold water
2 cups (1 pint) whipping or
    heavy cream
1 jar (7 ounces) roasted red
    peppers, drained and
    coarsely chopped
½ cup mayonnaise

1 cup chopped fresh basil
    leaves*
¼ cup grated Parmesan cheese
1 small clove garlic, finely
    chopped
½ teaspoon salt
⅛ teaspoon pepper
    Sliced Italian bread

In 2-cup glass measure, sprinkle unflavored gelatine over cold water; let stand 2 minutes. Microwave at HIGH (Full Power) 1 minute. Stir thoroughly, then let stand 2 minutes or until gelatine is completely dissolved.

In large bowl, with electric mixer, beat cream until soft peaks form. Gradually add roasted peppers, mayonnaise, basil, cheese, garlic, salt and pepper. While beating, gradually add lukewarm gelatine mixture and beat until blended. Pour into 7-cup mold or bowl; chill until firm, at least 3 hours. Unmold and serve with bread.

Makes about 6 cups spread

*Substitution: Use 1 cup chopped fresh parsley plus 1 teaspoon dried basil leaves.

CONVENTIONAL DIRECTIONS: Increase cold water to ½ cup. In small saucepan, sprinkle unflavored gelatine over cold water; let stand 1 minute. Stir over low heat until gelatine is completely dissolved, about 3 minutes. Remove from heat and let stand until lukewarm, about 2 minutes. Proceed as above.

GOLDEN CHICKEN NUGGETS

1 envelope Lipton Onion-
    Mushroom Recipe Soup Mix
¾ cup plain dry bread crumbs
1½ pounds boneless skinless
    chicken breasts, cut into
    1-inch pieces

3 tablespoons Imperial
    Margarine, melted

Combine onion-mushroom recipe soup mix with bread crumbs. Dip chicken in bread crumb mixture, coating well. In 2-quart microwave-safe shallow baking dish, arrange chicken, then drizzle with margarine. Microwave uncovered at HIGH (Full Power) 6 minutes or until chicken is done, rearranging chicken once.

Makes about 2 dozen nuggets

Cajun-Style Chicken Nuggets: Add 1½ teaspoons chili powder, 1 teaspoon ground cumin and ¼ teaspoon ground red pepper to bread crumb mixture.

Note: Recipe can be doubled.

CONVENTIONAL DIRECTIONS: Preheat oven to 400°. Prepare chicken as above. In lightly greased large shallow baking pan, arrange chicken, then drizzle with margarine. Bake, turning once, 10 minutes or until chicken is done.

CHILLED MELON SOUP

1 envelope Knox Unflavored
   Gelatine
½ cup cold water
¼ cup sugar
1½ cups orange juice
1 tablespoon lemon juice
1 teaspoon chopped fresh mint
   (optional)

3 cups coarsely chopped
   cantaloupe, honeydew or
   crenshaw melon (about
   1 medium)
¼ cup whipping or heavy cream
   (optional)

In 2-cup glass measure, sprinkle unflavored gelatine over cold water; let stand 2 minutes. Microwave at HIGH (Full Power) 1½ minutes; stir thoroughly, then let stand 2 minutes or until gelatine is completely dissolved. Stir in sugar until completely dissolved, then add orange juice, lemon juice and mint.

In blender or food processor, process melon with gelatine mixture until smooth. Pour into serving bowl. Stir in cream; chill about 3 hours. Stir before serving. Garnish, if desired, with additional fresh mint.   *Makes about 5 cups soup*

CONVENTIONAL DIRECTIONS: In medium saucepan, sprinkle unflavored gelatine over cold water; let stand 1 minute. Stir over low heat until gelatine is completely dissolved, about 3 minutes. Stir in sugar until completely dissolved, then add orange juice, lemon juice and mint. Proceed as above.

STUFFED MUSHROOMS

½ pound ground turkey
1 small onion, diced
1 teaspoon Lawry's Seasoned
   Salt
¼ cup seasoned dry bread
   crumbs

¼ teaspoon oregano leaves
¼ teaspoon Lawry's Garlic
   Powder with Parsley
½ cup shredded Monterey Jack
   cheese (2 ounces)
24 large mushrooms

In large microwave-safe bowl, cook ground turkey at HIGH (Full Power) 2½ minutes or until crumbly, stirring once; drain. Add onion, seasoned salt, bread crumbs, oregano, garlic powder with parsley and cheese; blend well.

Remove stems from mushrooms. Chop stems and add to meat mixture. Stuff mushroom caps with meat mixture. Place on microwave-safe dish; cover with wax paper. Microwave at HIGH 4 minutes or until mushrooms are tender. Sprinkle, if desired, with chopped parsley.   *Makes about 2 dozen appetizers*

CONVENTIONAL DIRECTIONS: Preheat oven to 350°. In medium skillet brown turkey over medium heat until crumbly; drain. Add onion; cook 1 minute. Add remaining ingredients except mushrooms. Remove stems from mushrooms. Chop stems and add to meat mixture. Stuff mushroom caps as above. Place in baking dish and bake covered 15 minutes or until mushrooms are tender.

ITALIAN-STYLE STUFFED ARTICHOKES

4 large artichokes (about 3 pounds)
4 cups fresh bread crumbs*
⅔ cup Wish-Bone Italian Dressing

½ cup chopped onion
2 tablespoons grated Parmesan cheese
2 tablespoons chopped parsley
1½ cups chicken broth

Prepare artichokes for cooking as directed; set aside.

In medium bowl, combine bread crumbs, Italian dressing, ¼ cup onion, cheese and parsley.

In 2-quart microwave-safe oblong baking dish, add artichokes, chicken broth and remaining ¼ cup onion. Cover with plastic wrap, venting one corner, and microwave at HIGH (Full Power) 13 to 15 minutes or until leaves are tender and pull out easily. Carefully remove artichokes and stuff bread crumb mixture between artichoke leaves. Return artichokes to baking dish; cover with vented plastic wrap and microwave at HIGH 8 minutes or until artichokes are tender, basting artichokes once.   *Makes 4 appetizer servings*

*For best flavor and texture, make fresh bread crumbs using Italian or French bread.

CONVENTIONAL DIRECTIONS: Increase dressing to ¾ cup and broth to 2 cups. Prepare artichokes and stuffing as above. Stuff bread crumb mixture between artichoke leaves. In large non-aluminum saucepan, bring chicken broth and remaining ¼ cup onion to a boil. Add artichokes and simmer covered, basting occasionally, 40 minutes or until leaves are tender and pull out easily.

● Also terrific with Wish-Bone Robusto Italian, Herbal Italian, Blended Italian, Italian & Cheese, Lite Italian, Olive Oil Vinaigrette or Lite Classic Dijon Vinaigrette Dressing.

How to Prepare Artichokes for Cooking
1. Wash artichokes in cold water; drain.
2. With a large knife, cut stem close to base. Cut off 1 inch of top.
3. Remove tough lower leaves or discolored leaves.
4. If desired, with scissors, cut off sharp leaf tips. Brush cut edges with lemon juice.

◆◆◆

SPRINGTIME NOODLES ALFREDO

2 tablespoons Imperial
    Margarine
2 medium carrots, sliced
1 medium zucchini or yellow
    squash, thinly sliced
1 medium clove garlic, finely
    chopped
1⅓ cups water

1 cup milk
1 package Lipton Noodles &
    Sauce - Alfredo
1 tablespoon snipped fresh dill*
½ cup frozen peas, thawed
    (optional)
Pepper to taste

In 1½-quart microwave-safe casserole, microwave margarine, carrots, zucchini and garlic, uncovered, at HIGH (Full Power) 6 minutes or until vegetables are tender, stirring once; remove and set aside. Into casserole, stir water, milk and noodles & Alfredo sauce. Microwave at HIGH 11 minutes or until noodles are tender. Stir in vegetables, dill, peas and pepper; cover and let stand 2 minutes. Sprinkle, if desired, with grated Parmesan cheese. *Makes about 4 servings*

*Substitution: Use ½ teaspoon dried dill weed.

CONVENTIONAL DIRECTIONS: In large skillet, melt margarine and cook carrots, zucchini and garlic over medium-high heat, stirring occasionally, 3 minutes or until vegetables are tender; remove and set aside. Into skillet, add water and milk and bring to the boiling point. Stir in noodles & Alfredo sauce and dill and continue boiling over medium heat, stirring occasionally, 7 minutes or until noodles are tender. Stir in vegetables, peas and pepper; heat through. Serve as above.

RATATOUILLE

2 tablespoons olive or vegetable
    oil
2 teaspoons finely chopped
    garlic
3 cups cubed peeled eggplant
    (about ½ medium)
1 cup chopped onion
1 cup sliced zucchini
1 cup chopped green pepper
1 can (14½ ounces) whole
    peeled tomatoes, undrained
    and chopped
¼ teaspoon oregano leaves
1½ cups water
1 package Lipton Rice &
    Sauce - Chicken Flavor
Salt and pepper to taste

In 2-quart microwave-safe round casserole, microwave oil with garlic, uncovered, at HIGH (Full Power) 30 seconds. Add eggplant, onion, zucchini and green pepper; microwave at HIGH 6 minutes or until vegetables are tender, stirring once. Add tomatoes and oregano and microwave at HIGH 5 minutes, stirring once. Stir in water and rice & chicken flavor sauce. Cover with plastic wrap, venting one corner, then microwave at HIGH 12 minutes or until rice is tender; stir in salt and pepper. Let stand covered 5 minutes.

Makes about 4 side-dish or 2 main-dish servings

CONVENTIONAL DIRECTIONS: Increase oregano to ½ teaspoon and decrease water to 1¼ cups. In large skillet, heat oil and cook garlic over medium heat 30 seconds. Add eggplant, onion, zucchini and green pepper and cook over medium-high heat, stirring frequently, 2 minutes or until vegetables are tender. Add tomatoes and oregano and cook covered, stirring occasionally, 20 minutes. Stir in water and rice & chicken flavor sauce and bring to a boil. Reduce heat and simmer covered, stirring occasionally, 10 minutes or until rice is tender; stir in salt and pepper.

CARROTS ELEGANTE

1 pound fresh carrots, thinly
    sliced*
¼ cup water
⅓ cup orange marmalade
1 tablespoon Imperial
    Margarine
½ teaspoon Lawry's Seasoned
    Salt

In 1½-quart microwave-safe casserole, microwave carrots with water, covered, at HIGH (Full Power) 7 to 8 minutes, stirring once; drain. Immediately stir in remaining ingredients.   *Makes about 5 servings*

*Substitution: Use 1 package (16 ounces) frozen crinkle-cut carrots.

CONVENTIONAL DIRECTIONS: Increase water to ½ cup. Into medium saucepan, pour ½ cup water. Set vegetable steamer in pan; bring water to a boil. Place carrots in steamer; cover and steam 10 minutes or until tender. Remove carrots to serving bowl; immediately stir in remaining ingredients.

SIMPLY GREEN BEANS

1 pound fresh green beans,
   ends removed and cut in
   half crosswise
¼ cup water
1 tablespoon Imperial
   Margarine, melted

¼ to ½ teaspoon Lawry's
   Seasoned Pepper
¼ teaspoon Lawry's Garlic
   Powder with Parsley
3 tablespoons grated Romano
   cheese

In microwave-safe shallow dish, place green beans and water. Cover with plastic wrap, venting one corner, and microwave at HIGH (Full Power) 14 to 16 minutes, stirring once; drain. Stir in margarine, seasoned pepper to taste and garlic powder with parsley; let stand covered 1 minute. Sprinkle with cheese.

Makes about 4 servings

CONVENTIONAL DIRECTIONS: Increase water to 2 quarts. In large saucepan, bring water to a boil; add beans. Bring water back to a boil and cook 4 minutes. Drain; rinse under cold running water. In medium skillet, melt margarine and cook green beans 3 minutes or until tender. Stir in remaining ingredients.

HOPPIN' JOHN RICE

4 slices bacon, cut into 1-inch
   pieces
6 ounces boneless pork,
   coarsely chopped (optional)
1 medium onion, chopped
1 teaspoon finely chopped
   garlic

2 cups water
1 package Lipton Rice & Sauce -
   Beef Flavor
1 can (16 ounces) black-eyed
   peas, rinsed and drained
2 dashes hot pepper sauce

In 2-quart microwave-safe casserole, microwave bacon with pork, uncovered, at HIGH (Full Power) 2 minutes or until cooked; remove. Reserve 1 tablespoon drippings. Add onion and garlic to reserved drippings and microwave at HIGH 2 minutes. Add water and rice & beef flavor sauce and microwave at HIGH 12 minutes or until rice is tender. Stir in black-eyed peas, hot pepper sauce, bacon and pork. Let stand covered 5 minutes. Top, if desired, with additional crisp-cooked crumbled bacon.

Makes about 4 servings

CONVENTIONAL DIRECTIONS: In medium saucepan, cook bacon with pork until well browned; remove. Reserve 1 tablespoon drippings. Add onion and garlic to reserved drippings and cook over medium heat 3 minutes or until tender. Add water and rice & beef flavor sauce and bring to a boil. Reduce heat and simmer, stirring occasionally, 10 minutes or until rice is tender. Stir in black-eyed peas, hot pepper sauce, bacon and pork; heat through. Serve as above.

ORIENTAL VEGETABLE STIR-FRY

⅓ cup Wish-Bone Italian
    Dressing
 1 tablespoon soy sauce
 1 teaspoon light brown sugar
¼ teaspoon ground ginger
½ pound snow peas (about
    2 cups)*

1 medium red pepper, chopped
1 can (15 ounces) whole baby
    corn, drained and cut into
    thirds

In 2-quart microwave-safe casserole, blend Italian dressing, soy sauce, brown sugar and ginger. Add remaining ingredients and toss to coat. Microwave uncovered at HIGH (Full Power) 6 minutes or until crisp-tender, stirring once.

Makes about 4 servings

*Variation: Use 2 cups broccoli florets.

CONVENTIONAL DIRECTIONS: In large skillet, blend Italian dressing as above. Heat, then add remaining ingredients and cook over medium-high heat, stirring occasionally, 6 minutes or until crisp-tender.

● Also terrific with Wish-Bone Robusto Italian, Blended Italian, Lite Italian or Herbal Italian Dressing.

HOMEMADE TOMATO SAUCE WITH PASTA

½ cup Wish-Bone Robusto
    Italian Dressing
½ cup chopped onions
 1 can (28 ounces) whole plum
    tomatoes, undrained and
    chopped

3 tablespoons chopped fresh
    basil leaves*
½ pound pasta, cooked and
    drained
    Grated Parmesan cheese

In 2-quart microwave-safe casserole, microwave robusto Italian dressing with onions, uncovered, at HIGH (Full Power) 3 minutes or until onions are tender. Add tomatoes and microwave at HIGH 20 minutes or until thickened; stir in basil. To serve, pour tomato sauce over hot pasta and sprinkle with cheese.

Makes 4 side-dish or 2 main-dish servings

*Substitution: Use 2 teaspoons dried basil leaves.

CONVENTIONAL DIRECTIONS: In large skillet, heat robusto Italian dressing and cook onions over medium heat, stirring occasionally, 3 minutes or until onions are tender. Add tomatoes and cook over medium heat 10 minutes or until thickened; stir in basil. Serve as above.

● Also terrific with Wish-Bone Italian, Blended Italian, Italian & Cheese, Lite Italian or Herbal Italian Dressing.

Oriental Vegetable Stir-Fry

PASTA PRIMAVERA

1 cup Wish-Bone Lite Italian
Dressing
½ cup finely chopped green
onions
Assorted Fresh Vegetables
4 medium tomatoes, chopped
¼ cup dry white wine (optional)
2 tablespoons finely chopped
fresh basil leaves (optional)

1 teaspoon Lawry's Seasoned
Salt
¼ teaspoon Lawry's Seasoned
Pepper
1 pound fettuccine noodles,
cooked and drained

In 3-quart microwave-safe casserole, microwave Italian dressing, green onions and carrots (if used), covered, at HIGH (Full Power) 4 minutes, stirring once. Add remaining Assorted Fresh Vegetables and microwave covered at HIGH 3½ minutes. Stir in tomatoes and microwave covered at HIGH 4 minutes or until vegetables are crisp-tender. Stir in wine, basil, seasoned salt and seasoned pepper and microwave uncovered at HIGH 2 minutes, stirring once. Toss with hot fettuccine. Sprinkle, if desired, with grated Parmesan cheese.   *Makes about 6 servings*

Assorted Fresh Vegetables: Use any combination of the following to equal 2 quarts—asparagus cut into 2-inch pieces, broccoli florets, sliced carrots, zucchini or yellow squash.

CONVENTIONAL DIRECTIONS: Increase wine to ½ cup. In large skillet, heat Italian dressing and cook green onions over medium heat 1 minute. Add tomatoes, then Assorted Fresh Vegetables and cook, stirring occasionally, 10 minutes or until vegetables are crisp-tender. Add wine, basil, seasoned salt and seasoned pepper and cook 2 minutes. Toss and sprinkle as above.

● Also terrific with Wish-Bone Italian, Robusto Italian, Italian & Cheese, Blended Italian, Herbal Italian or Classic Dijon Vinaigrette Dressing.

OVERSTUFFED POTATOES

6 large baking potatoes
1 cup milk
1 envelope Lipton Vegetable
Recipe Soup Mix

½ cup Imperial Margarine
¼ teaspoon pepper
½ cup shredded Cheddar cheese
(about 2 ounces)

Scrub potatoes, then pierce several times with fork. On microwave-safe plate, arrange potatoes and microwave at HIGH (Full Power) 18 to 21 minutes or until tender, turning potatoes over and rearranging once. Cover plate with aluminum foil; let stand 5 minutes. Meanwhile, in 2-cup glass measure, blend milk with vegetable recipe soup mix and microwave at HIGH 2 minutes or until hot; set aside.

Cut a lengthwise slice from top of each potato. Remove skin from the top slice and place pulp into medium bowl. Scoop pulp from each potato, leaving ¼-inch-thick shells; add to bowl. With electric mixer, beat potato pulp until fluffy. Add soup mixture, margarine and pepper and beat until well blended. Equally spoon potato filling into potato shells, then sprinkle with cheese. On microwave-safe plate, arrange potatoes. Microwave at HIGH 6 minutes or until heated through.
Makes 6 servings

CONVENTIONAL DIRECTIONS: Preheat oven to 425°. Scrub and pierce potatoes as above. Bake 1 hour or until tender. Meanwhile, in small saucepan, blend milk with vegetable recipe soup mix and cook over medium heat until heated through; set aside.

Prepare potato shells and filling and stuff potato shells as above. On baking sheet, arrange potatoes. Bake 15 minutes or until heated through.

SPAGHETTI SQUASH TOSS

2 tablespoons Imperial
    Margarine
1 cup sliced mushrooms
1 envelope Lipton Vegetable
    Recipe Soup Mix
1 cup (½ pint) light cream or
    half and half

¼ cup dry white wine
½ medium spaghetti squash,
    seeded and cooked
2 tablespoons grated Parmesan
    cheese

In 1½-quart microwave-safe casserole, microwave margarine with mushrooms, uncovered, at HIGH (Full Power) 2 minutes. Stir in vegetable recipe soup mix blended with cream and wine. Microwave uncovered at HIGH 5 minutes or until sauce is thickened, stirring once. Meanwhile, with fork, gently remove spaghetti-like strands from squash. Add squash and cheese to casserole and microwave uncovered at HIGH 1 minute or until heated through. Let stand covered 5 minutes. Serve, if desired, with additional cheese and freshly ground pepper.

Makes about 4 servings

Note: Recipe can be doubled.

CONVENTIONAL DIRECTIONS: In large saucepan, melt margarine and cook mushrooms over medium heat until tender. Stir in vegetable recipe soup mix blended with cream and wine. Bring just to the boiling point, then simmer, stirring occasionally, 5 minutes or until sauce is thickened. Meanwhile, prepare squash as above. Add squash and cheese to saucepan; toss well. Serve as above.

Easy Squash Cookery
Pierce squash with fork, then cook according to one of the following methods:
• *Cut squash in half. In microwave-safe oblong baking dish, place squash, cut-side down, and microwave at HIGH (Full Power), turning dish occasionally, 17 minutes or until fork-tender.*
• *Bake whole squash at 350°, 1 hour or until fork-tender.*
• *Place whole squash in large saucepan or stockpot; add water to cover. Boil 35 minutes or until fork-tender.*

◆◆◆

HOMESTYLE ZUCCHINI & TOMATOES

3 medium zucchini, thinly sliced (about 4½ cups)
1 can (14½ ounces) whole peeled tomatoes, drained and chopped (reserve liquid)

1 envelope Lipton Golden Onion Recipe Soup Mix
1 medium clove garlic, finely chopped*
½ teaspoon basil leaves

In 2-quart microwave-safe casserole, combine zucchini with tomatoes. Stir in golden onion recipe soup mix thoroughly blended with reserved liquid, garlic and basil. Microwave covered at HIGH (Full Power) 5 minutes, stirring once. Remove cover and microwave at HIGH 4 minutes or until zucchini is tender, stirring once. Let stand covered 2 minutes. *Makes about 4 servings*

*Substitution: Use ¼ teaspoon Lawry's Garlic Powder with Parsley.

CONVENTIONAL DIRECTIONS: In large skillet, heat 2 tablespoons oil and cook garlic with zucchini over medium-high heat 3 minutes. Stir in tomatoes, then golden onion recipe soup mix thoroughly blended with reserved liquid and basil. Bring to a boil, then simmer, stirring occasionally, 10 minutes or until zucchini is tender and sauce is slightly thickened.

• Also terrific with Lipton Onion Recipe Soup Mix.

GREEN BEAN CASSEROLE

4 slices bacon*
1 envelope Lipton Cream of Mushroom Cup-a-Soup Instant Soup
½ cup water
2 teaspoons dried minced onions

1 teaspoon Dijon-style mustard
1 package (10 ounces) frozen green beans
Pepper to taste

On microwave-safe rack or paper towel-lined plate, arrange bacon; cover with additional paper towel. Microwave at HIGH (Full Power) 3½ minutes or until crisp; remove bacon and crumble. In 1-quart microwave-safe casserole, with fork or wire whisk, blend instant cream of mushroom soup mix, water, onions and mustard; top with green beans. Microwave covered at HIGH 8 minutes, stirring once. Stir in bacon and pepper. *Makes about 4 servings*

*Substitution: Use 2 tablespoons bacon bits.

CONVENTIONAL DIRECTIONS: In medium skillet, cook bacon. Drain and crumble; set aside. Into skillet, add water, onions and green beans and bring to a boil. Simmer covered 5 minutes or until tender. Stir in instant cream of mushroom soup mix and mustard until smooth; stir in bacon and pepper.

Homestyle Zucchini & Tomatoes

GAZPACHO RICE

2 tablespoons Imperial
   Margarine
1 teaspoon finely chopped
   garlic
1 medium tomato, chopped
½ cup peeled, seeded and
   chopped cucumber
½ cup sliced green onions

2 cups water
1 package Lipton Rice &
   Sauce - Spanish
1 tablespoon finely chopped
   fresh coriander (cilantro)
Lawry's Seasoned Pepper to
   taste

In 1½-quart microwave-safe casserole, microwave margarine with garlic, uncovered, at HIGH (Full Power) 25 seconds. Stir in tomato, cucumber and green onions and microwave at HIGH 1 minute. Stir in water and rice & Spanish sauce and microwave at HIGH 12 minutes or until rice is tender. Stir in coriander and pepper. Let stand covered 5 minutes. *Makes about 4 servings*

CONVENTIONAL DIRECTIONS: In medium saucepan, melt margarine and cook garlic over medium heat 30 seconds. Stir in tomato, cucumber and green onions and cook over medium heat 1 minute. Add water and rice & Spanish sauce and bring to a boil. Reduce heat and simmer, stirring occasionally, 10 minutes or until rice is tender. Stir in coriander and pepper.

NO-FUSS RISOTTO

2½ cups chicken broth
  4 tablespoons Wish-Bone
    Blended Italian Dressing

½ cup chopped onions
1 cup uncooked arborio rice*
⅓ cup grated Parmesan cheese

In 4-cup glass measure, microwave chicken broth at HIGH (Full Power) 6 minutes or until boiling; set aside. In 2-quart microwave-safe casserole, microwave 3 tablespoons blended Italian dressing with onions, uncovered, at HIGH 3 minutes or until onions are tender. Stir in uncooked rice, coating well; stir in hot chicken broth. Microwave covered at HIGH 6 minutes or until boiling, then microwave covered at MEDIUM (50% Power) 12 minutes or until rice is tender. Stir in remaining 1 tablespoon dressing and cheese. Let stand 2 minutes, then serve immediately. Garnish, if desired, with chopped parsley.

Makes about 4 servings

*Substitution: Use 1 cup uncooked regular rice.

CONVENTIONAL DIRECTIONS: Add 2¼ cups water. In large saucepan, bring chicken broth and 2¼ cups water to a boil, then simmer. Meanwhile, in large skillet, heat 3 tablespoons blended Italian dressing with onions and cook over medium heat, stirring occasionally, 3 minutes or until onions are tender. Stir in uncooked rice, coating well; cook 2 minutes, stirring frequently. Add a ladleful of broth mixture, stirring rice constantly until broth is absorbed. Repeat, stirring constantly, until rice is tender, about 30 minutes. Stir in remaining 1 tablespoon dressing and cheese. Serve and garnish as above.

● Also terrific with Wish-Bone Italian and Herbal Italian Dressing.

SICILIAN SPAGHETTI SQUASH

2 tablespoons Imperial
   Margarine
½ cup minced onion
¼ cup diced green pepper
1 jar (2 ounces) diced pimiento
1 large spaghetti squash,
   seeded and cooked (see
   page 31)
1 teaspoon Lawry's Seasoned
   Salt

1 teaspoon Lawry's Garlic Salt
½ teaspoon Lawry's Seasoned
   Pepper
2 cups shredded Monterey Jack
   cheese (about 6 ounces)
1 can (2¼ ounces) sliced pitted
   ripe olives, drained

In small microwave-safe dish, microwave margarine, onion and green pepper, uncovered, at HIGH (Full Power) 1 to 2 minutes or until tender; add pimiento. With fork, gently remove spaghetti-like strands from squash. In 1½-quart microwave-safe baking dish, combine squash, green pepper mixture and remaining ingredients. Microwave at HIGH 2 minutes or until cheese is melted.

Makes about 6 servings

CONVENTIONAL DIRECTIONS: Preheat oven to 350°. In small skillet, melt margarine and cook onion and green pepper until tender; add pimiento. With fork, gently remove spaghetti-like strands from squash. In 1½-quart baking dish, combine squash, green pepper mixture and remaining ingredients. Bake 5 minutes or until heated through and cheese is melted.

BROCCOLI AU GRATIN

1 cup water
1 envelope Lipton Golden Onion
   or Onion Recipe Soup Mix
3 tablespoons all-purpose flour
1 cup milk
1 teaspoon Worcestershire
   sauce

1 cup shredded Cheddar cheese
   (about 4 ounces)
1 medium bunch broccoli or
   1 medium head cauliflower,
   separated into large florets
   and cooked*
Paprika

In 1½-quart microwave-safe casserole, microwave water at HIGH (Full Power) 5 minutes. Stir in golden onion recipe soup mix and microwave covered at HIGH 3 minutes. Stir in flour blended with milk and Worcestershire sauce. Microwave uncovered at HIGH 3 minutes or until sauce is thickened, stirring once. Stir in cheese until melted. Add broccoli and microwave covered at HIGH 2 minutes or until heated through. Let stand covered 5 minutes. Sprinkle with paprika.

Makes about 6 servings

*Substitution: Use 2 packages (10 ounces each) frozen broccoli spears or cauliflower, cooked and drained.

CONVENTIONAL DIRECTIONS: Preheat oven to 375°. In medium saucepan, bring water to a boil; stir in golden onion recipe soup mix and simmer covered 5 minutes. Stir in flour blended with milk and Worcestershire sauce. Bring just to the boiling point, then simmer, stirring constantly, until sauce is thickened, about 5 minutes. Stir in cheese until melted. In 2-quart casserole, arrange broccoli; top with cheese sauce. Bake 15 minutes or until heated through. Sprinkle with paprika.

TERRIFIC POTATO TOPPER

2 envelopes Lipton Onion Cup-
    a-Soup Instant Soup
1 container (8 ounces) sour
    cream

4 medium baking potatoes
4 slices bacon*

In small bowl, blend instant onion soup mix with sour cream; set aside. Scrub potatoes, then pierce several times with fork. On microwave-safe plate, arrange potatoes and microwave at HIGH (Full Power) 14 to 17 minutes or until tender, turning potatoes over and rearranging once. Cover plate with aluminum foil; let stand 5 minutes. Meanwhile, on microwave-safe rack or paper-towel-lined plate, arrange bacon; cover with additional paper towel. Microwave at HIGH 3½ minutes or until bacon is crisp. Crumble bacon and stir into sour cream mixture.

Cut each potato in half lengthwise almost completely through; mash pulp lightly. To serve, evenly top each potato with sour cream mixture.   *Makes 4 servings*

*Substitution: Use 2 tablespoons bacon bits.

CONVENTIONAL DIRECTIONS: Preheat oven to 425°. Blend instant onion soup mix and pierce potatoes as above. Bake potatoes 45 to 60 minutes or until tender. Meanwhile, in medium skillet, cook bacon; remove and crumble. Stir bacon into sour cream mixture. Cut and serve potatoes as above.

QUICK SEASONED VEGETABLES

1 envelope Lipton Cream of
    Chicken Flavor Cup-a-Soup
    Instant Soup
⅓ cup water

1 package (10 ounces) frozen
    peas, green beans, chopped
    broccoli or mixed
    vegetables

In 1-quart microwave-safe casserole, with fork or wire whisk, blend instant cream of chicken flavor soup mix with water; top with vegetables. Microwave covered at HIGH (Full Power) 7 minutes or until tender, stirring once.

Makes about 4 servings

CONVENTIONAL DIRECTIONS: In medium saucepan, bring vegetables and water to a boil. Simmer covered 4 minutes or until tender. Stir in instant cream of chicken flavor soup mix until smooth.

Terrific Potato Topper (right) and Quick Seasoned Vegetables (left)

MAIN DISHES

ZESTY ZUCCHINI LASAGNA

1 package (1.5 ounces) Lawry's Spaghetti Sauce Seasoning Blend with Imported Mushrooms
1 can (6 ounces) tomato paste
1¾ cups water
2 tablespoons Imperial Margarine
1 pound ground beef
½ teaspoon basil leaves
⅛ teaspoon thyme leaves
2 cups ricotta cheese
1 egg, slightly beaten
4 medium zucchini, thinly sliced lengthwise
1 cup shredded mozzarella cheese (about 4 ounces)

In 1-quart glass measure, combine spaghetti sauce seasoning blend with imported mushrooms, tomato paste, water and margarine. Cover with wax paper and microwave at HIGH (Full Power) 15 minutes, stirring every 4 minutes. In 1-quart microwave-safe casserole, place ground beef. Microwave at HIGH 5 minutes or until no longer pink, stirring once. Drain fat; crumble beef. Stir in prepared spaghetti sauce, basil and thyme; set aside. In small bowl, combine ricotta cheese with egg. In 12×8-inch microwave-safe casserole, arrange zucchini; sprinkle with water. Cover with plastic wrap, venting one corner, and microwave at HIGH 2 minutes; drain liquid. In same dish, layer ½ of the zucchini, ricotta mixture and meat sauce. Repeat layers. Cover with plastic wrap, venting one corner, and microwave at HIGH 14 minutes, turning casserole once. Sprinkle with mozzarella cheese; microwave uncovered at HIGH 3 minutes or until cheese is melted.

Makes about 6 servings

CONVENTIONAL DIRECTIONS: Preheat oven to 350°. In medium saucepan, brown ground beef until no longer pink; drain. Into saucepan, stir spaghetti sauce seasoning blend with imported mushrooms, tomato paste, water, margarine, basil and thyme. Bring to a boil, then simmer uncovered 10 minutes. In small bowl, combine ricotta cheese with egg; set aside. In medium saucepan, bring 1 quart water to a boil. Add zucchini and cook 2 minutes; remove and rinse under cold running water. In 12×8-inch casserole, layer as above. Top with mozzarella cheese and bake uncovered 30 minutes or until cheese is melted.

SALMON WITH ZUCCHINI & CARROT RIBBONS

3 tablespoons Imperial
  Margarine
½ cup sliced green onions
2 cups water
1 package Lipton Noodles &
  Sauce - Butter
1 small zucchini, peeled in
  lengthwise strips*
1 small carrot, peeled in
  lengthwise strips*

2 tablespoons snipped fresh
  dill**
2 tablespoons plus 1 teaspoon
  lemon juice
Pepper to taste
4 salmon fillets (about
  1½ pounds)
Salt to taste

In 1½-quart microwave-safe casserole, microwave 1 tablespoon margarine with green onions, uncovered, at HIGH (Full Power) 2 minutes. Stir in water and noodles & butter sauce and microwave at HIGH 12 minutes or until noodles are tender. Stir in zucchini, carrot, 1 tablespoon dill, 1 teaspoon lemon juice and pepper. Microwave at HIGH 1 minute; cover and set aside.

In 2-quart microwave-safe oblong casserole, arrange salmon with thickest portions to outer edge of casserole. Evenly top with remaining 2 tablespoons margarine, cut into small pieces, 2 tablespoons lemon juice, remaining 1 tablespoon dill, salt and additional pepper. Cover with plastic wrap, venting one corner, and microwave at HIGH 5 minutes or until salmon flakes easily. Let stand covered 2 minutes. Serve with noodles and garnish, if desired, with sliced lemon and additional dill.

Makes about 4 servings

*Hint: Use vegetable peeler to easily make vegetable ribbons.

**Substitution: Use 2 teaspoons dried dill weed.

CONVENTIONAL DIRECTIONS: Increase margarine to 4 tablespoons. In medium saucepan, melt 2 tablespoons margarine and cook green onions over medium heat 1 minute. Add water and bring to a boil. Stir in noodles & butter sauce and continue boiling over medium heat, stirring occasionally, 6 minutes or until noodles are almost tender. Stir in zucchini, carrot, 1 tablespoon dill, 1 teaspoon lemon juice and pepper. Cook, stirring frequently, 1 minute or until noodles are tender.

Meanwhile, on large broiler pan, arrange salmon. Evenly dot with remaining 2 tablespoons margarine, cut into small pieces, 2 tablespoons lemon juice, 1 tablespoon dill, salt and additional pepper. Broil 5 minutes or until salmon flakes easily. Serve and garnish as above.

Melting Butter or Margarine
In small microwave-safe bowl, microwave at HIGH (Full Power):

2 tablespoons – 40 seconds
4 tablespoons – 1 minute
8 tablespoons – 1 to 2 minutes

◆◆◆

SEAFOOD OVER ANGEL HAIR PASTA

⅓ cup Wish-Bone Italian
  Dressing
¼ cup chopped shallots or
  onions
1 cup thinly sliced carrots
4 ounces snow peas, thinly
  sliced (about 1 cup)
¾ cup chicken broth
3 tablespoons sherry
½ pound uncooked medium
  shrimp, cleaned (keep tails
  on)

½ pound sea scallops
8 mussels, well scrubbed
¼ cup whipping or heavy cream
2 tablespoons all-purpose flour
  Salt and pepper to taste
8 ounces angel hair pasta or
  capellini, cooked and
  drained

In 3-quart microwave-safe casserole, microwave Italian dressing, shallots and carrots, covered, at HIGH (Full Power) 3 minutes, stirring once. Add snow peas and microwave covered at HIGH 2 minutes. Add chicken broth and sherry and microwave covered at HIGH 2½ minutes or until boiling. Add shrimp, scallops and mussels. Microwave covered at HIGH 5 minutes or until seafood is done and mussel shells open, stirring once. (Discard any unopened shells.) Stir in cream blended with flour and microwave uncovered at MEDIUM (50% Power) 1 minute or until sauce is slightly thickened. Stir in salt and pepper. Serve over hot pasta and sprinkle, if desired, with freshly ground pepper and grated Parmesan cheese.

Makes about 4 servings

CONVENTIONAL DIRECTIONS: Decrease Italian dressing to ¼ cup. Increase chicken broth to 1 cup and sherry to ¼ cup. In 12-inch skillet, heat Italian dressing and cook shallots over medium-high heat 2 minutes. Add carrots and snow peas and cook 2 minutes. Add broth, then sherry. Bring to a boil, then add shrimp, scallops and mussels. Simmer covered 3 minutes or until seafood is done and mussel shells open. (Discard any unopened shells.) Stir in cream blended with flour and cook over medium heat, stirring occasionally, 2 minutes or until sauce is slightly thickened. Stir in salt and pepper. Serve as above.

● Also terrific with Wish-Bone Robusto Italian, Italian & Cheese, Herbal Italian, Blended Italian, Classic Dijon Vinaigrette, Olive Oil Vinaigrette or Lite Classic Dijon Vinaigrette Dressing.

SLOPPY JOES

1 pound ground beef
2 envelopes Lipton Onion Cup-
  a-Soup Instant Soup

1 can (8 ounces) tomato sauce
2 teaspoons sugar
½ teaspoon prepared mustard

In 1½-quart microwave-safe casserole, microwave ground beef, uncovered, at HIGH (Full Power) 3 minutes or until no longer pink, stirring once; drain. Stir in remaining ingredients and microwave at HIGH 4 minutes, stirring once. Serve on toasted hamburger rolls.

Makes about 4 servings

CONVENTIONAL DIRECTIONS: In medium skillet, brown ground beef; drain. Stir in remaining ingredients and simmer 5 minutes or until heated through. Serve as above.

Seafood over Angel Hair Pasta

FILLET STUFFED WITH CRABMEAT

1 envelope Lipton Golden Onion
    Recipe Soup Mix
½ cup fresh bread crumbs
1 package (6 ounces) frozen
    crabmeat, thawed and
    drained
1 hard-cooked egg, coarsely
    chopped

½ cup water
2 teaspoons lemon juice
⅛ teaspoon ground nutmeg
4 fish fillets (about 1 pound)
1 tablespoon butter or
    margarine, melted

In medium bowl, combine golden onion recipe soup mix, bread crumbs, crabmeat, egg, water, lemon juice and nutmeg.

Evenly top fillets with crabmeat mixture; roll up and secure with wooden toothpicks. Place in lightly greased 2-quart microwave-safe oblong baking dish. Brush fish with butter and microwave at HIGH (Full Power) 10 minutes or until fish flakes easily, turning dish once. *Makes 4 servings*

CONVENTIONAL DIRECTIONS: Preheat oven to 350°. Prepare fish as above. Bake 25 minutes or until fish flakes easily.

CHICKEN & RICE ENCHILADAS

1 tablespoon Imperial
    Margarine
¼ cup chopped green onions
1¾ cups water
1 package Lipton Rice &
    Sauce - Spanish
1 can (16 ounces) refried beans

1 cup shredded Monterey Jack
    cheese (about 3 ounces)
1 medium tomato, chopped
1 can (4 ounces) chopped green
    chilies, drained
1 cup cut-up cooked chicken
6 flour tortillas, softened

In 1½-quart microwave-safe oblong baking dish, microwave margarine with green onions, uncovered, at HIGH (Full Power) 2 minutes. Stir in water and rice & Spanish sauce and microwave at HIGH 10 minutes. Stir in beans, cheese, tomato, chilies and chicken. Evenly spread 1 cup rice mixture on each tortilla. Roll and place on serving plate. Serve, if desired, with taco sauce, sour cream and guacamole. *Makes about 6 servings*

Variation: Place rolled tortillas in 13×9-inch microwave-safe baking dish. Top with ⅔ cup taco sauce or salsa and 1 cup shredded Monterey Jack cheese. Cover with wax paper and microwave at HIGH 7 minutes, turning dish every 2 minutes. Let stand 5 minutes.

CONVENTIONAL DIRECTIONS: In medium saucepan, melt margarine and cook green onions until tender. Stir in water and rice & Spanish sauce; bring to a boil. Reduce heat and simmer, stirring occasionally, 9 minutes. Stir in beans, cheese, tomato, chilies and chicken. Evenly spread 1 cup rice mixture on each tortilla. Roll and place on serving plate. Serve as above.

Variation: Preheat oven to 375°. Prepare rice mixture as above. Evenly spread 1 cup rice mixture on each tortilla. Roll and place seam-side down in 13×9-inch baking dish; top with ⅔ cup taco sauce or salsa. Bake 10 minutes. Top with 1 cup shredded Monterey Jack cheese; bake an additional 5 minutes.

SHRIMP ALFREDO WITH RICOTTA CHEESE

3 cups broccoli florets
2 tablespoons butter or
    margarine
1 tablespoon finely chopped
    garlic
1 pound uncooked medium
    shrimp, cleaned*

1½ cups water
1 cup milk
1 package Lipton Noodles &
    Sauce - Alfredo
1 cup ricotta cheese
Pepper to taste

In 2-quart microwave-safe casserole, microwave broccoli, butter and garlic, uncovered, at HIGH (Full Power) 1 minute. Add shrimp and microwave at HIGH 3 minutes or until shrimp turn pink and broccoli is crisp-tender, stirring once; remove and set aside. Into casserole, add water, milk and noodles & Alfredo sauce. Microwave uncovered at HIGH 11 minutes or until noodles are tender, stirring once. Stir in ricotta, shrimp mixture and pepper. Microwave at HIGH 2 minutes or until heated through. Let stand covered 2 minutes.   *Makes about 4 servings*

*Substitution: Use 1 pound boneless skinless chicken breasts, cut into strips and seasoned with salt and pepper. Microwave at HIGH 4 minutes after adding to broccoli mixture.

CONVENTIONAL DIRECTIONS: Increase butter to ¼ cup and decrease water to 1¼ cups. In large skillet, melt butter and cook garlic over medium-high heat 30 seconds. Add shrimp and broccoli and cook, stirring occasionally, 4 minutes or until shrimp turn pink and broccoli is crisp-tender; remove and set aside. Into skillet, add water and milk and bring to the boiling point. Stir in noodles & Alfredo sauce and continue boiling over medium heat, stirring occasionally, 8 minutes or until noodles are tender. Stir in ricotta, shrimp mixture and pepper; heat through.

CREAMY CHICKEN CASSEROLE

1 cup cut-up cooked chicken
1 can (7 ounces) whole kernel
    corn, drained
1 cup milk
2 envelopes Lipton Creamy
    Broccoli Cup-a-Soup Instant
    Soup

⅛ teaspoon thyme leaves
1½ cups hot cooked mashed
    potatoes
1 cup shredded Swiss cheese
    (about 4 ounces)

In 1-quart microwave-safe casserole, combine chicken with corn; set aside. In 2-cup glass measure or small microwave-safe bowl, with fork or wire whisk, blend milk, instant creamy broccoli soup mix and thyme. Microwave uncovered at HIGH (Full Power) 4 minutes or until thickened, stirring once. Pour soup mixture over chicken and corn; top with potatoes, then cheese. Microwave uncovered at HIGH 3 minutes or until heated through. Sprinkle, if desired, with paprika.
Makes about 2 servings

CONVENTIONAL DIRECTIONS: Preheat oven to 400°. In 1-quart casserole, combine chicken with corn; set aside. In small saucepan, with fork or wire whisk, blend milk, instant creamy broccoli soup mix and thyme. Bring just to the boiling point, stirring occasionally, then simmer 3 minutes or until thickened. Pour soup mixture over chicken and corn; top with potatoes, then cheese. Bake 10 minutes or until heated through.

QUICK AND EASY TAMALE PIE

½ pound ground beef
¼ cup sliced green onions
2 envelopes Lipton Tomato Cup-a-Soup Instant Soup
¼ cup water
1 can (7 ounces) whole kernel corn, drained
2 tablespoons chopped pitted ripe olives (optional)

¼ teaspoon chili powder
3 slices (¾ ounces each) American cheese, halved
2 corn muffins, cut into ½-inch cubes
Mexican Sour Cream Topping (optional)

In shallow microwave-safe 1-quart casserole, microwave ground beef with green onions at HIGH (Full Power) 2½ minutes or until beef is no longer pink, stirring once. Stir in instant tomato soup mix, water, corn, olives and chili powder until well blended. Top with cheese, then evenly spread muffin cubes over cheese. Microwave at HIGH 5 minutes or until heated through and cheese is melted, turning casserole once. Garnish, if desired, with fresh coriander (cilantro), sliced pitted ripe olives and jalapeño peppers. Serve with Mexican Sour Cream Topping.

Makes 2 main-dish or 4 snack-size servings

Mexican Sour Cream Topping: Blend ½ cup sour cream, 2 tablespoons chopped jalapeño peppers and 1 teaspoon lime juice.

Note: Recipe can be doubled. Prepare in a 2-quart microwave-safe shallow casserole and microwave ground beef 6 minutes or until no longer pink, stirring twice. Increase the final cooking time to 8 minutes or until heated through and cheese is melted.

CONVENTIONAL DIRECTIONS: Increase water to ½ cup. In medium skillet, brown ground beef. Stir in instant tomato soup mix, water, corn, green onions, olives and chili powder until well blended. Top with cheese and muffin cubes as above. Cook 5 minutes or until heated through and cheese is melted. Garnish as above.

Covering Up

A tight cover, such as dish lids or vented plastic wrap, holds steam and moisture inside — great for vegetables, fruits, casseroles, chicken breasts and fish.

Microwave-safe paper towels absorb grease and moisture, allow steam to escape and prevent fats from splattering — great for cooking bacon, reheating breads, cakes or items with a crisp crust.

Wax paper allows steam to escape while preventing splattering — great for foods that splatter and meats that do not need tenderizing.

◆◆◆

ORIENTAL CHICKEN WITH VEGETABLES

½ pound boneless skinless
    chicken breasts, cut into
    thin strips
1½ cups frozen mixed vegetables,
    thawed
2 envelopes Lipton Cream of
    Chicken Flavor Cup-a-Soup
    Instant Soup

1 cup water
2 teaspoons soy sauce
¼ teaspoon Lawry's Garlic
    Powder with Parsley
¼ teaspoon ground ginger
    Dash crushed red pepper
1½ cups hot cooked rice

In 2-quart microwave-safe casserole, microwave chicken, uncovered, at HIGH (Full Power) 2 minutes or until almost done. Add vegetables, then instant cream of chicken flavor soup mix blended with water, soy sauce, garlic powder with parsley and ginger. Microwave at HIGH 5 minutes or until sauce thickens. Stir in red pepper. Let stand uncovered 2 minutes. Serve over hot rice.

Makes about 2 servings

CONVENTIONAL DIRECTIONS: Add 1 tablespoon oil. In medium skillet, heat oil and cook chicken until almost done; remove. Add vegetables, then instant cream of chicken flavor soup mix blended with water, soy sauce, garlic powder with parsley and ginger. Bring to a boil, then simmer, stirring occasionally, 5 minutes or until sauce thickens. Add chicken and red pepper; heat through. Serve as above.

SHRIMP CREOLE

1 can (14½ ounces) whole
    peeled tomatoes, undrained
    and chopped
½ cup Wish-Bone Italian
    Dressing
1 medium green pepper, cut into
    chunks

1 medium onion, sliced
1 pound uncooked medium
    shrimp, cleaned
⅛ teaspoon crushed red pepper
2 cups hot cooked rice

Discard ½ cup liquid from tomatoes. In 1½-quart microwave-safe casserole, microwave Italian dressing, green pepper and onion, covered, at HIGH (Full Power) 4 minutes or until tender, stirring once. Add tomatoes with remaining liquid and microwave covered at HIGH 5 minutes. Add shrimp and red pepper and microwave covered at HIGH 3 minutes or until shrimp turn pink, stirring once. To serve, arrange shrimp mixture over hot rice. *Makes about 4 servings*

CONVENTIONAL DIRECTIONS: In medium skillet, heat Italian dressing and cook green pepper and onion over medium heat, stirring occasionally, 5 minutes or until tender. Stir in tomatoes with liquid and simmer covered 15 minutes. Add shrimp and red pepper and simmer covered an additional 5 minutes or until shrimp turn pink. Serve as above.

● Also terrific with Wish-Bone Robusto Italian, Lite Italian, Italian & Cheese or Herbal Italian Dressing.

Oriental Chicken with Vegetables

GARLIC SHRIMP WITH NOODLES

4 tablespoons butter
¼ cup finely chopped onion
2 cups water
1 package Lipton Noodles & Sauce - Butter & Herb
2 tablespoons olive oil
1 tablespoon finely chopped garlic

1 pound uncooked medium shrimp, cleaned
1 can (14 ounces) artichoke hearts, drained and halved
¼ cup finely chopped parsley
Pepper to taste

In 2-quart microwave-safe casserole, microwave 2 tablespoons butter with onion, uncovered, at HIGH (Full Power) 2 minutes or until tender. Stir in water and noodles & butter & herb sauce and microwave at HIGH 11 minutes or until noodles are tender. Stir, then cover and set aside.

In 1-quart microwave-safe casserole or 9-inch glass pie plate, microwave remaining 2 tablespoons butter, oil and garlic at HIGH 2 minutes. Stir in shrimp and artichokes and microwave covered at HIGH 3 minutes or until shrimp are almost pink, stirring once; stir in parsley and pepper. Combine shrimp mixture with noodles and microwave covered at HIGH 1 minute or until heated through. Let stand covered 2 minutes. *Makes about 4 servings*

CONVENTIONAL DIRECTIONS: In medium saucepan, melt 2 tablespoons butter and cook onion until tender. Add water and bring to a boil. Stir in noodles & butter & herb sauce and continue boiling over medium heat, stirring occasionally, 8 minutes or until noodles are tender. Meanwhile, in large skillet, heat remaining 2 tablespoons butter with oil and cook garlic over medium-high heat 30 seconds. Add shrimp and artichokes and cook, stirring occasionally, 3 minutes or until shrimp turn pink. Stir in parsley and pepper.

SIMPLE SUPPER ESPAÑOL

2 envelopes Lipton Tomato Cup-a-Soup Instant Soup
2 teaspoons chili powder
1 teaspoon Lawry's Garlic Salt
2 cups water
½ cup uncooked regular rice

1 pound ground beef
½ cup chopped onion
⅓ cup diced green pepper
2 slices bacon, crisp-cooked and crumbled
Shredded Cheddar cheese

In 2-quart microwave-safe casserole, blend instant tomato soup mix, chili powder, garlic salt and water. Stir in uncooked rice and microwave covered at HIGH (Full Power) 12 minutes. Stir in ground beef, onion and green pepper; microwave covered at HIGH 10 minutes or until rice is tender. Stir in bacon; top with cheese. Let stand covered 5 minutes. *Makes about 4 servings*

CONVENTIONAL DIRECTIONS: In medium skillet, brown ground beef with onion and green pepper; drain. Stir in uncooked rice and instant tomato soup mix, chili powder and garlic salt blended with water. Bring to a boil, then simmer covered 20 minutes or until rice is tender. Stir in bacon; top with cheese.

Garlic Shrimp with Noodles

SAVORY ORANGE CHICKEN

2 pounds chicken pieces
Pepper to taste
1 cup sliced mushrooms
1 teaspoon finely chopped
   garlic
½ cup orange juice

½ cup dry white wine
1 cup water
1 teaspoon grated orange peel
   (optional)
1 envelope Lipton Rice & Sauce
   - Chicken Flavor

Trim excess fat from chicken pieces, then season with pepper. In 2-quart microwave-safe casserole, arrange chicken skin-side down and cover with wax paper. Microwave at HIGH (Full Power) 10 minutes, turning chicken once. Remove chicken; drain. In same casserole, microwave mushrooms with garlic, uncovered, at HIGH 1½ minutes, stirring once. Stir in orange juice, wine, water, orange peel and rice & chicken flavor sauce. Microwave uncovered at HIGH 5 minutes. Arrange chicken pieces on rice with thickest portions to outer edge of casserole. Microwave uncovered at HIGH 7 minutes or until rice is tender and chicken is done. Garnish, if desired, with orange slices and finely chopped parsley.

Makes about 4 servings

CONVENTIONAL DIRECTIONS: Add 2 tablespoons oil. Trim chicken and season as above. In large skillet, heat oil and cook garlic over medium heat 30 seconds. Add chicken and cook over medium-high heat until browned; drain. Add orange juice, wine and orange peel. Simmer covered, stirring occasionally, 20 minutes or until chicken is done; remove chicken. Into skillet, stir water, rice & chicken flavor sauce and mushrooms; bring to a boil. Reduce heat and simmer, stirring occasionally, 7 minutes or until rice is tender and sauce is desired consistency. Add chicken; heat through. Garnish as above.

LIPTON ONION BURGERS

1 envelope Lipton Onion Recipe
Soup Mix

2 pounds ground beef
½ cup water

In large bowl, combine all ingredients; shape into 8 patties. Place 4 patties in microwave-safe oblong baking dish and microwave uncovered at HIGH (Full Power) 6 minutes, turning patties once. Repeat with remaining patties. Let stand covered 5 minutes. Serve, if desired, with toasted hamburger buns.

Makes 8 servings

Tempting Taco Burgers: Add 2 teaspoons chili powder to ground beef mixture. Microwave as above. Top with shredded lettuce, Cheddar cheese and chopped tomatoes.

CONVENTIONAL DIRECTIONS: Prepare patties as above. Grill or broil until done. Serve as above.

• Also terrific with Lipton Beefy Onion or Beefy Mushroom Recipe Soup Mix.

Savory Orange Chicken

CHICKEN BREASTS FLORENTINE

2 pounds boneless skinless
   chicken breasts
¼ cup all-purpose flour
2 eggs, well beaten
⅔ cup seasoned dry bread
   crumbs
1 medium clove garlic, finely
   chopped
1 envelope Lipton Golden Onion
   Recipe Soup Mix

1½ cups water
¼ cup dry white wine
2 tablespoons finely chopped
   parsley
⅛ teaspoon pepper
   Hot cooked rice pilaf or white
   rice
   Hot cooked spinach

Dip chicken in flour, then eggs, then bread crumbs. In 3-quart microwave-safe casserole, microwave chicken, uncovered, at HIGH (Full Power) 4 minutes, rearranging chicken once. Add garlic, then stir in golden onion recipe soup mix thoroughly blended with water and wine. Microwave uncovered 5 minutes or until boiling, stirring once. Microwave uncovered at MEDIUM (50% Power), stirring occasionally, 7 minutes or until chicken is done and sauce is slightly thickened. Stir in parsley and pepper. Let stand covered 5 minutes. To serve, arrange chicken over hot rice and spinach; garnish as desired. *Makes about 6 servings*

CONVENTIONAL DIRECTIONS: Add ¼ cup oil and increase wine to ½ cup. Dip chicken as above. In large skillet, heat ¼ cup oil and cook chicken over medium heat until almost done; remove and set aside. Reserve 1 tablespoon drippings. Add garlic and wine to reserved drippings and cook over medium heat 5 minutes. Stir in golden onion recipe soup mix thoroughly blended with water; bring to a boil. Return chicken to skillet and simmer covered 10 minutes or until chicken is done and sauce is slightly thickened. Stir in parsley and pepper. Serve as above.

Standing Time
Many microwave-cooked foods need standing time because they continue to cook after being removed from the oven. The larger the amount of food, the longer the standing time.

◆◆◆

GOBBLER BURGERS

1 pound ground turkey
2 envelopes Lipton Onion Cup-
   a-Soup Instant Soup
1 egg
⅓ cup plain dry bread crumbs

1 teaspoon Worcestershire
   sauce
½ teaspoon Lawry's Garlic Salt
¼ teaspoon thyme leaves
   (optional)

In medium bowl, combine all ingredients; shape into 4 patties. On microwave-safe plate, arrange patties and microwave uncovered at HIGH (Full Power) 7 minutes, turning patties once. Serve, if desired, with whole berry cranberry sauce on toasted whole wheat rolls. *Makes 4 servings*

CONVENTIONAL DIRECTIONS: Prepare patties as above. Grill or broil until done. Serve as above.

Chicken Breasts Florentine

TURKEY PARMIGIANA

1 package (1.5 ounces) Lawry's
    Spaghetti Sauce Seasoning
    Blend with Imported
    Mushrooms
1 can (6 ounces) tomato paste
2¼ cups water
2 tablespoons Imperial
    Margarine

½ cup unseasoned dry bread
    crumbs
¼ cup plus 3 tablespoons grated
    Parmesan cheese
1 pound sliced turkey cutlets*
1 egg, beaten
1 cup shredded mozzarella
    cheese (about 4 ounces)

In 1-quart glass measure, blend spaghetti sauce seasoning blend with imported mushrooms, tomato paste, water and margarine. Cover with wax paper and microwave at HIGH (Full Power) 15 minutes, stirring every 4 minutes. In shallow bowl or plate, combine bread crumbs with ¼ cup Parmesan cheese. Dip each turkey cutlet in beaten egg, then coat with crumb mixture. Place turkey cutlets in 13 × 9-inch microwave-safe baking dish. Cover with wax paper and microwave at MEDIUM-HIGH (70% Power) 5 minutes. Rearrange turkey; cover and microwave at MEDIUM-HIGH 2 minutes. Top with prepared spaghetti sauce. Sprinkle with mozzarella cheese and remaining 3 tablespoons Parmesan cheese. Cover with wax paper and microwave at MEDIUM-HIGH 3 minutes or until sauce is hot and cheese is melted.
Makes about 4 servings

*Substitution: Use 1 pound boneless skinless chicken breasts or veal cutlets.

CONVENTIONAL DIRECTIONS: Preheat oven to 350°. Increase margarine to 4 tablespoons. Prepare spaghetti sauce seasoning blend with imported mushrooms with tomato paste, water and 2 tablespoons margarine according to package directions. In shallow bowl or plate, combine bread crumbs with ¼ cup Parmesan cheese. Dip each turkey cutlet in beaten egg, then coat with crumb mixture. In large skillet, melt 2 tablespoons margarine and brown turkey cutlets. Place browned turkey cutlets in 13 × 9-inch baking dish and top with prepared spaghetti sauce. Sprinkle with mozzarella cheese and remaining 3 tablespoons Parmesan cheese. Bake covered 25 minutes or until sauce is hot and cheese is melted.

SOUPERIOR MEAT LOAF

1 envelope Lipton Onion Recipe
    Soup Mix
2 pounds ground beef
1½ cups fresh bread crumbs

2 eggs
¾ cup water
⅓ cup ketchup

In large bowl, combine all ingredients. In 2-quart microwave-safe oblong baking dish, shape into loaf. Microwave uncovered at HIGH (Full Power), turning dish occasionally, 25 minutes or until done; drain. Let stand covered 5 minutes.
Makes about 8 servings

CONVENTIONAL DIRECTIONS: Preheat oven to 350°. Combine as above. In large baking pan, shape into loaf. Bake 1 hour or until done.

● Also terrific with Lipton Beefy Onion, Onion-Mushroom or Beefy Mushroom Recipe Soup Mix.

Turkey Parmigiana and Warm Spinach Salad (see page 9)

POACHED SALMON STEAKS

⅓ cup chopped onion
⅓ cup chopped carrots
⅓ cup chopped celery
1 quart water
½ cup dry white wine

1 teaspoon Lawry's Seasoned
   Salt
6 black peppercorns
2 salmon steaks (½ to
   ¾ pound each)

In 13 × 9-inch microwave-safe dish, combine all ingredients except salmon. Cover with plastic wrap, venting one corner, and microwave at HIGH (Full Power) 8 minutes. Place salmon in hot liquid; cover with vented plastic wrap and microwave at HIGH 4½ minutes or until salmon flakes easily. Let stand covered 3 minutes before removing. Strain vegetables and serve over salmon. (Cooking liquid may be used for fish soup or stew.) Serve hot or cold. Garnish, if desired, with lemon slices and fresh dill. *Makes about 2 servings*

CONVENTIONAL DIRECTIONS: In large skillet, combine all ingredients except salmon; bring just to a boil. Place salmon in hot liquid. Cook covered over medium-low heat 8 minutes or until salmon flakes easily. Serve as above.

CARIBBEAN COCONUT CHICKEN NUGGETS

¾ cup flaked coconut
½ cup plain dry bread crumbs
¼ teaspoon ground cumin
1 envelope Lipton Cream of
   Chicken Flavor Cup-a-Soup
   Instant Soup
⅓ cup water

1 teaspoon lime juice
¼ teaspoon hot pepper sauce
1 pound boneless skinless
   chicken breasts, cut into
   1-inch pieces*
Honey-Mustard Dipping Sauce

On 9-inch microwave-safe plate, combine coconut, bread crumbs and cumin. Microwave uncovered at HIGH (Full Power) 2½ minutes or until golden. Meanwhile, in small bowl, with wire whisk or fork, blend instant cream of chicken flavor soup mix, water, lime juice and hot pepper sauce; let stand 2 minutes to thicken. Stir chicken into soup mixture, coating well, then add to coconut mixture, coating well.

Place chicken in 2-quart microwave-safe oblong baking dish and microwave uncovered at HIGH 5 minutes or until done. Serve with Honey-Mustard Dipping Sauce. *Makes about 4 servings*

*Substitution: Use 1 pound uncooked shrimp, cleaned.

Honey-Mustard Dipping Sauce: In small bowl, blend ⅓ cup Dijon-style mustard with ⅓ cup honey.

CONVENTIONAL DIRECTIONS: In shallow dish, combine coconut, bread crumbs and cumin. In small bowl, blend soup mixture as above. Stir chicken into soup mixture, coating well, then add to coconut mixture, coating well. Broil 8 minutes or until chicken is done, turning chicken once. Serve as above.

Poached Salmon Steaks and Simply Green Beans (see page 27)

CHICKEN WITH POTATOES & PEPPERS

1 chicken (2½ to 3 pounds), cut into serving pieces
1 pound all-purpose potatoes, cut into 1-inch chunks
1 can (28 ounces) whole peeled tomatoes, drained and chopped (reserve ½ cup liquid)
½ cup Wish-Bone Italian Dressing

2 medium onions, cut into quarters
2 medium red, green or yellow peppers, cut into thin strips
1 tablespoon fresh rosemary leaves*
1 teaspoon thyme leaves
1 teaspoon salt
¼ teaspoon pepper

In 3-quart microwave-safe casserole, arrange chicken skin-side down with thickest portions to outer edge of casserole. Cover with wax paper and microwave at HIGH (Full Power) 12 minutes, rearranging once; drain. Remove chicken and place on paper towels; set aside. In same casserole, microwave potatoes, tomatoes and reserved liquid, covered, at HIGH 15 minutes or until potatoes are tender, stirring once. Add remaining ingredients. Microwave covered at HIGH 8 minutes, stirring once. Arrange chicken on vegetable mixture skin-side up with thickest portions to outer edge of casserole. Microwave covered at HIGH 6 minutes or until chicken is done. Serve, if desired, with French or Italian bread. *Makes about 4 servings*

*Substitution: Use 1 teaspoon dried rosemary leaves.

CONVENTIONAL DIRECTIONS: Preheat oven to 375°. Reserve all the juice from whole peeled tomatoes. In large skillet, heat Italian dressing and brown chicken over medium-high heat; set aside. In 13×9-inch baking pan, combine remaining ingredients; add chicken and turn to coat. Bake uncovered, stirring occasionally, 50 minutes or until chicken is done and vegetables are tender. Serve as above.

● Also terrific with Wish-Bone Robusto Italian, Blended Italian, Lite Italian, Herbal Italian, Italian & Cheese, Classic Dijon Vinaigrette or Lite Classic Dijon Vinaigrette Dressing.

SAVORY TUNA PUFFS

1 egg, slightly beaten
1 envelope Lipton Spring Vegetable Cup-a-Soup Instant Soup
1 can (6½ ounces) tuna, drained and flaked

1 to 2 tablespoons mayonnaise
2 English muffins, split and toasted
4 slices American cheese

In medium bowl, blend egg with instant spring vegetable soup mix. Stir in tuna and mayonnaise. On microwave-safe plate, place each muffin half. Top with cheese slice and ¼ cup tuna mixture. Microwave at HIGH (Full Power) 1 minute or until tuna mixture puffs and cheese is melted. *Makes 4 puffs*

CONVENTIONAL DIRECTIONS: Preheat oven or toaster oven to 400°. Prepare tuna mixture as above. On baking tray, place each muffin half. Top with cheese slice and ¼ cup tuna mixture. Bake 10 minutes or until tuna mixture puffs and cheese is melted.

Chicken with Potatoes & Peppers

CHINESE-STYLE BEEF & VEGETABLES

⅓ cup Wish-Bone Italian
  Dressing
1 tablespoon soy sauce
¼ teaspoon ground ginger
1 cup very thinly sliced carrots

1 cup sliced mushrooms
1 cup sliced zucchini
1½ pounds boneless sirloin steak,
  cut into thin strips
4 cups hot cooked rice

In small bowl, blend Italian dressing, soy sauce and ginger; reserve 2 tablespoons. In 2-quart microwave-safe round casserole, microwave remaining dressing mixture with carrots, uncovered, at HIGH (Full Power) 6 minutes or until carrots are crisp-tender, stirring once. Add mushrooms and zucchini and microwave covered 2½ minutes or until crisp-tender. Remove vegetables and keep warm. Into casserole, add reserved dressing mixture and beef. Microwave uncovered at HIGH 5 minutes or until beef is tender, stirring once. Return vegetables to casserole and microwave at HIGH 1 minute or until heated through. To serve, arrange beef and vegetables over hot rice.   *Makes about 6 servings*

CONVENTIONAL DIRECTIONS: In small bowl, blend Italian dressing and reserve as above. In large skillet, heat remaining dressing mixture and cook carrots, covered, over medium heat, stirring occasionally, 10 minutes. Add mushrooms and zucchini and cook covered an additional 5 minutes or until crisp-tender. Remove vegetables and keep warm. Into skillet, add reserved dressing mixture and beef. Cook uncovered over high heat, stirring constantly, 5 minutes or until beef is tender. Return vegetables to skillet and heat through. Serve as above.

● Also terrific with Wish-Bone Robusto Italian, Blended Italian, Herbal Italian, Lite Italian, Classic Dijon Vinaigrette or Lite Classic Dijon Vinaigrette Dressing.

MARINATED SHRIMP ITALIANO

⅓ cup Wish-Bone Italian
  Dressing

1 pound uncooked medium
  shrimp, cleaned

In 9-inch microwave-safe pie plate, combine Italian dressing with shrimp. Cover and marinate in refrigerator, turning occasionally, at least 2 hours. Arrange shrimp around outer edge of pie plate; cover with plastic wrap, venting one corner. Microwave at HIGH (Full Power) 2½ minutes or until shrimp turn pink, rearranging after 2 minutes. Let stand covered 2 minutes. Serve, if desired, over hot cooked rice and garnish with chopped fresh coriander (cilantro) or parsley.
    Makes about 4 servings

CONVENTIONAL DIRECTIONS: In large shallow non-aluminum broiler-proof pan, marinate shrimp as above. Broil shrimp with dressing, turning and basting frequently, 5 minutes or until shrimp turn pink. Serve as above.

● Also terrific with Wish-Bone Robusto Italian, Olive Oil Vinaigrette or Herbal Italian Dressing.

Chinese-Style Beef & Vegetables

BEAT-THE-HEAT CHEESECAKE

2 envelopes Knox Unflavored
   Gelatine
1 cup cold water
2 packages (8 ounces each)
   cream cheese, softened
1 cup (8 ounces) creamed
   cottage cheese

¾ cup sugar
1 cup (½ pint) whipping or
   heavy cream
1 tablespoon vanilla extract
   Graham Cracker Almond Crust

In 2-cup glass measure, sprinkle unflavored gelatine over ½ cup cold water; let stand 2 minutes. Microwave at HIGH (Full Power) 1½ minutes. Stir thoroughly, then let stand 2 minutes or until gelatine is completely dissolved.

With electric mixer, combine cream cheese, cottage cheese and sugar until smooth. Stir in cream, remaining ½ cup water and vanilla until thoroughly blended. While mixer is running, gradually add gelatine mixture; beat 5 minutes or until mixture is smooth. Turn into Graham Cracker Almond Crust; chill until firm, about 5 hours. Garnish, if desired, with fruit.

Makes 1 cheesecake or 12 servings

Graham Cracker Almond Crust: In small bowl, combine 1 cup graham cracker crumbs, ½ cup ground almonds, 2 tablespoons sugar, ¼ cup melted Imperial Margarine and ½ teaspoon almond extract. Press onto bottom and sides of 9-inch springform pan; chill.

CONVENTIONAL DIRECTIONS: In small saucepan, sprinkle unflavored gelatine over ½ cup cold water; let stand 1 minute. Stir over low heat until gelatine is completely dissolved, about 5 minutes. Proceed as above.

FROZEN RASPBERRY DESSERT
WITH CHOCOLATE SAUCE

1 envelope Knox Unflavored
 Gelatine
¼ cup cold water
2 packages (10 ounces each)
 frozen raspberries in light
 syrup, thawed
½ cup cranberry-raspberry juice
 or cranberry juice cocktail

¼ cup sugar
1 teaspoon lemon juice
¾ cup frozen whipped topping,
 thawed
Chocolate Sauce

In 1-cup glass measure, sprinkle unflavored gelatine over cold water; let stand 2 minutes. Microwave at HIGH (Full Power) 40 seconds. Stir thoroughly, then let stand 2 minutes or until gelatine is completely dissolved.

In blender or food processor, process raspberries; strain to remove seeds, then return to processor. While processing, through feed cap, gradually add cranberry-raspberry juice, gelatine mixture, sugar and lemon juice. Pour into large bowl and chill, stirring occasionally, until mixture mounds slightly when dropped from spoon, about 30 minutes. Fold in whipped topping. Pour into 8½×4½×2-inch loaf pan; freeze 6 hours or until firm. Unmold onto platter and serve with Chocolate Sauce. Garnish, if desired, with fresh raspberries and mint leaves.

Makes 8 servings

CONVENTIONAL DIRECTIONS: In small saucepan, sprinkle unflavored gelatine over cold water; let stand 1 minute. Stir over low heat until gelatine is completely dissolved, about 3 minutes. Proceed as above.

Chocolate Sauce: In 2-cup glass measure, microwave 1 cup (½ pint) whipping or heavy cream with 1 package (6 ounces) semi-sweet chocolate chips at HIGH (Full Power) 2 minutes, stirring after 1 minute. Stir until chocolate is melted.

CONVENTIONAL DIRECTIONS: In medium saucepan, bring 1 cup (½ pint) whipping or heavy cream just to the boiling point. Remove from heat, then stir in 1 package (6 ounces) semi-sweet chocolate chips until melted.

Note: Prepare Chocolate Sauce ½ hour before serving, or prepare ahead of time and chill. To serve, microwave sauce at HIGH 1 minute; stir.

FRUIT JUICE KNOX BLOX

4 envelopes Knox Unflavored
 Gelatine

4 cups cold fruit juice

In 2-cup glass measure, sprinkle unflavored gelatine over 1 cup cold juice; let stand 3 minutes. Microwave at HIGH (Full Power) 1 minute 20 seconds; stir thoroughly. Let stand 2 minutes or until gelatine is completely dissolved. Pour into 8- or 9-inch baking dish; stir in remaining 3 cups juice. Chill until firm, about 3 hours. Cut into 1-inch squares.

Makes about 6 dozen blox

CONVENTIONAL DIRECTIONS: In small saucepan, heat 3 cups juice to boiling. Meanwhile, in large bowl, sprinkle unflavored gelatine over remaining 1 cup juice; let stand 1 minute. Add hot juice and stir until gelatine is completely dissolved, about 5 minutes. Pour into baking dish and chill as above.

EASY CHOCOLATE MOUSSE

1 envelope Knox Unflavored
   Gelatine
¼ cup cold water
2 tablespoons Imperial
   Margarine, softened
1¼ cups milk

½ cup sugar
⅓ cup unsweetened cocoa
   powder
1 teaspoon vanilla extract
1½ cups frozen whipped topping,
   thawed

In 1-cup glass measure, sprinkle unflavored gelatine over cold water; let stand 2 minutes. Microwave at HIGH (Full Power) 40 seconds. Stir thoroughly, then let stand 2 minutes or until gelatine is completely dissolved. Stir in margarine until melted.

Meanwhile, in blender or food processor, process milk, sugar, cocoa powder and vanilla until blended. While processing, through feed cap, gradually add gelatine mixture and process until blended. Pour into medium bowl, then with wire whisk or rotary beater, blend in whipped topping. Pour into dessert dishes or 4-cup bowl; chill until set, about 2 hours. Garnish, if desired, with additional whipped topping and chocolate curls. *Makes about 8 servings*

CONVENTIONAL DIRECTIONS: In small saucepan, sprinkle unflavored gelatine over cold water; let stand 1 minute. Stir over low heat until gelatine is completely dissolved, about 2 minutes. Stir in margarine until melted. Proceed as above.

FRESH FRUIT PARFAITS

1 envelope Knox Unflavored
   Gelatine
1¾ cups cold water
9 packets Equal® Sweetener or
   3 tablespoons sugar
⅓ cup fresh lemon juice (about
   2 lemons)

1 medium peach or nectarine,
   sliced
1 medium banana, sliced
1½ cups seedless green grapes,
   halved
1½ cups sliced strawberries

In 4-cup glass measure or microwave-safe medium bowl, sprinkle unflavored gelatine over ½ cup cold water; let stand 2 minutes. Microwave at HIGH (Full Power) 1½ minutes. Stir thoroughly, then let stand 2 minutes or until gelatine is completely dissolved. Stir in sweetener until dissolved, then add lemon juice and remaining 1¼ cups water.

In large bowl, combine fruit. Into six 8-ounce parfait or dessert glasses, evenly divide fruit. Evenly pour gelatine mixture over fruit to cover; chill until firm, about 3 hours. *Makes 6 servings*

CONVENTIONAL DIRECTIONS: In medium saucepan, sprinkle unflavored gelatine over ½ cup cold water; let stand 1 minute. Stir over low heat until gelatine is completely dissolved, about 3 minutes. Stir in sweetener until dissolved, then add lemon juice and remaining 1¼ cups water. Proceed as above.

CHOCOLATE-PECAN & CARAMEL PIE

1 envelope Knox Unflavored
    Gelatine
¼ cup cold water
2 cups (1 pint) whipping or
    heavy cream
1 package (6 ounces) semi-
    sweet chocolate chips

2 eggs
1 teaspoon vanilla extract
1 cup caramels (about 22)
2 tablespoons butter, cut into
    pieces
Chocolate-Pecan Crust

In 2-cup glass measure, sprinkle unflavored gelatine over cold water; let stand 2 minutes. Microwave at HIGH (Full Power) 40 seconds. Stir thoroughly, then let stand 2 minutes or until gelatine is completely dissolved. Stir in 1 cup cream. Microwave 2 minutes or until mixture comes to the boiling point, then immediately add to blender with chocolate. Process until chocolate is completely melted. While processing, through feed cap, add ½ cup cream, eggs and vanilla; process until blended. Pour into large bowl and chill until thickened, about 15 minutes.

Meanwhile, in 1-quart microwave-safe bowl, combine caramels with ¼ cup cream. Microwave at HIGH 1 minute; stir thoroughly. Microwave at HIGH an additional 1 minute, stirring once. Stir in butter until smooth. Pour onto Chocolate-Pecan Crust to cover bottom; let cool about 10 minutes.

With wire whisk or spoon, beat gelatine mixture until smooth. Pour into prepared crust; chill until firm, about 3 hours. Garnish with remaining ¼ cup cream, whipped, and, if desired, pecans. *Makes about 8 servings*

CONVENTIONAL DIRECTIONS: In small saucepan, sprinkle unflavored gelatine over cold water; let stand 1 minute. Stir over low heat until gelatine is completely dissolved, about 3 minutes. Stir in 1 cup cream. Bring just to the boiling point, then immediately add to blender with chocolate. Process until chocolate is completely melted. While processing, through feed cap, add ½ cup cream, eggs and vanilla; process until blended. Pour into large bowl and chill until thickened, about 15 minutes.

Meanwhile, in small saucepan, combine caramels, ¼ cup cream and butter. Simmer over low heat, stirring occasionally, until caramels are completely melted and mixture is smooth. Pour onto Chocolate-Pecan Crust to cover bottom; let cool about 10 minutes. With wire whisk or spoon, beat gelatine mixture until smooth. Pour into prepared crust; chill until firm, about 3 hours. Garnish as above.

Chocolate-Pecan Crust: In 10-inch microwave-safe pie plate, microwave ½ cup Imperial Margarine at HIGH (Full Power) 1 minute or until melted. Stir in 1 box (8½ ounces) chocolate wafer cookies, crumbled (about 2 cups crumbs) and ¾ cup finely chopped pecans. Press onto bottom and up sides to form high rim. Microwave 2 minutes, turning dish once; cool.

CONVENTIONAL DIRECTIONS: Preheat oven to 350°. In small bowl, combine 1 box (8½ ounces) chocolate wafer cookies, crumbled (about 2 cups crumbs), ¾ cup finely chopped pecans and ½ cup melted Imperial Margarine. Press into 9- or 10-inch pie pan and press up sides to form high rim. Bake 10 minutes; cool.

BLUSHING POACHED PEACHES

1 cup cold water
4 Lipton Special Blends
   Blackberry Tea Bags
½ cup sugar

2 tablespoons lemon juice
⅛ teaspoon ground nutmeg
4 peaches, halved and pitted

In 2-cup glass measure, microwave water with blackberry tea bags at HIGH (Full Power) 2 minutes or until very hot. (Tea should not boil.) Let stand 5 minutes. Remove tea bags.

In 2-quart microwave-safe baking dish, combine tea, sugar, lemon juice and nutmeg. Add peaches, cut-side down. Cover with plastic wrap, venting one corner, and microwave at HIGH 4 minutes or until peaches are tender, turning halfway through cooking time. Let stand covered 5 minutes. Remove peaches, reserving liquid; set aside peaches to cool. Microwave reserved liquid at HIGH 5 minutes or until slightly thickened.

Meanwhile, peel peaches, then pour thickened liquid over them. Serve, if desired, with ice cream. *Makes about 4 servings*

CONVENTIONAL DIRECTIONS: Substitute 1 cup boiling water for cold water. In teapot, pour 1 cup boiling water over blackberry tea bags. Cover and brew 5 minutes. Remove tea bags. In 4-quart heavy saucepan, combine tea, sugar, lemon juice and nutmeg. Add peaches, cut-side down. Simmer covered 10 minutes or until peaches are tender, turning after 5 minutes. Remove peaches, reserving liquid; set aside peaches to cool. Boil reserved liquid 3 minutes or until slightly thickened. Meanwhile, peel peaches. Serve as above.

Poached Apples: Substitute 4 tart red apples for peaches. Core and remove a strip of peel from top and bottom of apples. Pierce remaining peel around each apple to prevent splitting. Increase microwave cooking time to 7 minutes (conventional cooking time to 15 minutes), turning apples twice. Thicken reserved liquid and serve as above.

NO-BAKE OLD-FASHIONED COCONUT CREAM PIE

2 envelopes Knox Unflavored
   Gelatine
¼ cup cold water
1 can (15 ounces) cream of
   coconut
1 cup (½ pint) light cream or
   half and half

3 eggs*
9-inch baked pastry shell or
   graham cracker crust
4 cups whipped cream or
   whipped topping
2 tablespoons coconut, toasted

In 1-cup glass measure, sprinkle unflavored gelatine over cold water; let stand 2 minutes. Microwave at HIGH (Full Power) 40 seconds. Stir thoroughly, then let stand 2 minutes or until gelatine is completely dissolved.

In blender or food processor, process cream of coconut, light cream and eggs until blended. While processing, through feed cap, gradually add gelatine mixture and process until blended. Chill blender container until mixture is slightly thickened, about 15 minutes. Pour into pastry shell; chill until firm, about 3 hours. Top with whipped cream and coconut. *Makes 1 pie or 12 servings*

*Substitution: Use ¾ cup frozen cholesterol-free egg product, 1½ tablespoons Imperial Margarine and ⅛ teaspoon salt.

CONVENTIONAL DIRECTIONS: In small saucepan, sprinkle unflavored gelatine over cold water; let stand 1 minute. Stir over low heat until gelatine is completely dissolved, about 3 minutes. Proceed as above.

Toasting Coconut
On 9-inch microwave-safe pie plate, evenly spread ½ cup flaked coconut. Microwave at MEDIUM-HIGH (70% Power) 3 minutes or until golden, tossing with a fork every minute.

◆◆◆

CINNAMON FRUIT TART
WITH SOUR CREAM FILLING

1 envelope Knox Unflavored
    Gelatine
¼ cup cold water
1 cup (8 ounces) creamed
    cottage cheese
½ cup canned pineapple juice
½ cup sour cream
½ cup milk

¼ cup sugar
1 teaspoon lemon juice
    Cinnamon Graham Cracker
    Crust
    Suggested Fresh Fruit
2 tablespoons orange or apricot
    marmalade, melted

In 1-cup glass measure, sprinkle unflavored gelatine over cold water; let stand 2 minutes. Microwave at HIGH (Full Power) 40 seconds. Stir thoroughly, then let stand 2 minutes or until gelatine is completely dissolved.

In blender or food processor, process cottage cheese, pineapple juice, sour cream, milk, sugar and lemon juice until blended. While processing, through feed cap, gradually add gelatine mixture and process until blended. Pour into Cinnamon Graham Cracker Crust; chill until firm, about 3 hours. To serve, top with Suggested Fresh Fruit, then brush with marmalade. *Makes 1 tart or 12 servings*

CONVENTIONAL DIRECTIONS: Preheat oven to 375°. In small bowl, combine 2 cups graham cracker crumbs, 1 tablespoon sugar, ½ teaspoon ground cinnamon and ½ cup melted Imperial Margarine. Press into 10-inch tart pan. Bake 8 minutes; cool.

Cinnamon Graham Cracker Crust: In 10-inch microwave-safe quiche dish or pie plate, microwave ½ cup Imperial Margarine at HIGH (Full Power) 45 seconds or until melted. Stir in 2 cups graham cracker crumbs, 1 tablespoon sugar and ½ teaspoon ground cinnamon. Press firmly onto bottom and up sides of dish. Microwave 1½ minutes; cool.

CONVENTIONAL DIRECTIONS: Preheat oven to 375°. In small bowl, combine 2 cups graham cracker crumbs, 1 tablespoon sugar, ½ teaspoon ground cinnamon and ½ cup melted Imperial Margarine. Press into 10-inch tart pan. Bake 8 minutes; cool.

Suggested Fresh Fruit: Use any combination of the following to equal 2 cups— sliced strawberries, kiwi or oranges; blueberries or raspberries.

CINNAMON APPLE COFFEECAKE

1½ cups cold water
5 Lipton Cinnamon Apple
   Herbal Tea Bags
½ cup confectioners sugar
1 cup all-purpose flour
½ cup sugar
6 tablespoons Imperial
   Margarine, melted

1 egg
1 teaspoon baking powder
¼ teaspoon salt
¼ cup golden raisins
1 cup chopped apples
½ cup chopped walnuts
½ teaspoon grated lemon peel

In 2-cup glass measure, microwave water with cinnamon apple herbal tea bags at HIGH (Full Power) 3 minutes or until very hot. (Tea should not boil.) Let stand 5 minutes. Remove tea bags.

In 1-quart microwave-safe casserole, blend ¾ cup tea with confectioners sugar. Chill remaining tea at least 10 minutes. Microwave tea-sugar mixture 10 minutes or until thick and syrupy; let cool.

In large bowl, combine remaining chilled tea, flour, sugar, margarine, egg, baking powder and salt. With electric mixer or rotary beater, beat to moisten, then beat at medium speed 2 minutes. Fold in raisins and ½ cup apples. Spread into greased and wax-paper-lined 8-inch microwave-safe baking pan. Microwave uncovered at MEDIUM (50% Power) 8 minutes, turning casserole once. Microwave at HIGH (Full Power) 3 minutes or until done. Cake will look slightly wet and pull slightly away from sides of baking dish. Let stand 10 minutes. Garnish, if desired, with apple slices.

In small bowl, combine tea-sugar glaze with remaining ½ cup apples, walnuts and lemon peel. Spoon over warm cake and serve.   *Makes about 8 servings*

CONVENTIONAL DIRECTIONS: Preheat oven to 375°. Substitute 1½ cups boiling water for cold water. In teapot, pour 1½ cups boiling water over cinnamon apple herbal tea bags. Cover and brew 5 minutes. Remove tea bags. In 1-quart saucepan, combine ¾ cup tea with confectioners sugar. Chill remaining tea at least 10 minutes. Boil tea-sugar mixture over medium-high heat 7 minutes or until thick and syrupy. In large bowl, beat cake batter as above. Spread into greased 8-inch round cake pan. Bake 25 minutes or until toothpick inserted in center comes out clean. On wire rack, cool 10 minutes. Garnish as above. Prepare glaze and spoon over cake as above.

Toasting Nuts
On microwave-safe plate or paper towel, evenly spread 1 cup nuts.
Microwave at HIGH (Full Power) 2½ to 4 minutes or until toasted and fragrant, stirring twice.

◆◆◆

ZINFANDEL SORBET WITH POACHED PEARS

ZINFANDEL SORBET
1 envelope Knox Unflavored
   Gelatine
½ cup cold water

⅓ cup sugar
1¼ cups white Zinfandel wine
1 can (5½ ounces) pear nectar

In 2-cup glass measure, sprinkle unflavored gelatine over cold water; let stand 2 minutes. Microwave at HIGH (Full Power) 1½ minutes. Stir thoroughly, then let stand 2 minutes or until gelatine is completely dissolved. Stir in sugar until completely dissolved. In 9-inch square baking pan, combine gelatine mixture with remaining ingredients; freeze 3 hours or until firm.

With electric mixer or food processor, beat mixture until smooth. Return to pan; freeze 6 hours or until firm. Serve in Poached Pears drizzled with Poached Pear syrup. Garnish, if desired, with fresh mint. *Makes 8 servings*

CONVENTIONAL DIRECTIONS: In medium saucepan, sprinkle unflavored gelatine over cold water; let stand 1 minute. Stir over low heat until gelatine is completely dissolved, about 3 minutes. Stir in sugar until dissolved, then stir in remaining ingredients. Pour into 9-inch square baking pan; freeze 3 hours or until firm. With electric mixer or food processor, beat mixture until smooth, then freeze and serve as above.

POACHED PEARS
1¾ cups white Zinfandel wine
¾ cup sugar
1 tablespoon lemon juice

4 medium Anjou or Bartlett
   pears, peeled, halved and
   cored

In 2-quart microwave-safe round casserole, combine wine, sugar and lemon juice. Microwave at HIGH (Full Power) 5 minutes, stirring once. Add pears, turning to coat evenly. Cover with plastic wrap, venting one corner, and microwave at HIGH 6 minutes or until pears are fork-tender, turning pears over once. Remove pears and chill. Microwave remaining liquid, uncovered, at HIGH 9 minutes or until liquid is reduced by half; chill. *Makes 8 pear halves and about 1 cup syrup*

CONVENTIONAL DIRECTIONS: Increase wine to 2 cups. In large skillet, thoroughly blend wine, sugar and lemon juice. Add pear halves cut-side down and simmer covered 15 minutes or until pears are tender. Remove pears and chill. Cook remaining liquid, uncovered, over medium-high heat 10 minutes or until liquid is reduced by half; chill.

Hint: One bottle (750 ml) white Zinfandel wine is enough to make this entire recipe.

Melting Chocolate
In 2-cup glass measure or microwave-safe bowl, microwave 1 cup (6-ounce
package) semi-sweet chocolate chips at MEDIUM (50% Power) 2 minutes.
Chips will retain their shape even while soft. Stir, then microwave 30 seconds.
Terrific for dipping strawberries!

◆◆◆

STRAWBERRIES 'N CREAM FOOL

1 envelope Knox Unflavored
    Gelatine
¼ cup cold water
1 package (10 ounces) frozen
    strawberries in light syrup,
    thawed
¼ cup frozen orange juice
    concentrate, partially
    thawed and undiluted

¼ cup sugar
1 teaspoon finely chopped
    crystallized ginger
    (optional)
1 container (8 ounces) frozen
    whipped topping, thawed*

In 1-cup glass measure, sprinkle unflavored gelatine over cold water; let stand 2 minutes. Microwave at HIGH (Full Power) 40 seconds. Stir thoroughly, then let stand 2 minutes or until gelatine is completely dissolved.

In blender or food processor, process strawberries, orange juice concentrate, sugar and ginger. While processing, through feed cap, gradually add gelatine mixture and process until blended. In large bowl, blend 1 cup strawberry mixture with whipped topping. Pour into serving bowl. Gently fold in remaining strawberry mixture, just until marbled; chill until set, about 2 hours. Serve, if desired, with angel food or pound cake.
Makes 8 servings

*Substitution: Use 1 cup (½ pint) whipping or heavy cream, whipped.

CONVENTIONAL DIRECTIONS: In medium saucepan, sprinkle unflavored gelatine over cold water; let stand 1 minute. Stir over low heat until gelatine is completely dissolved, about 3 minutes. Proceed as above.

FRESH 'N FRUITY POPS

1 envelope Knox Unflavored
    Gelatine
½ cup cold water
1 cup fruit juice

Suggested Fresh Fruit
¼ cup sugar or 6 packets Equal®
    sweetener
1 tablespoon lemon juice

In 4-cup glass measure, sprinkle unflavored gelatine over cold water; let stand 2 minutes. Microwave at HIGH (Full Power) 1½ minutes. Stir thoroughly, then let stand 2 minutes or until gelatine is completely dissolved. Stir in remaining ingredients. Pour into 4 (5-ounce) popsicle molds or paper cups; freeze until partially frozen, about 30 minutes. Insert wooden ice cream sticks; freeze until firm, about 4 hours. To serve, let stand at room temperature 5 minutes; remove from molds.
Makes 4 pops

Suggested Fresh Fruit: Use any of the following, pureed, to equal 1 cup— bananas, blueberries, pitted cherries, cantaloupe, nectarines, peaches, plums or strawberries.

CONVENTIONAL DIRECTIONS: In small saucepan, sprinkle unflavored gelatine over cold water; let stand 1 minute. Stir over low heat until gelatine is completely dissolved, about 5 minutes. Stir in remaining ingredients. Pour into molds and freeze as above.

IT'S-A-SNAP CHEESECAKE

1 envelope Knox Unflavored
  Gelatine
1 cup cold water
2 packages (8 ounces each)
  cream cheese, softened

½ cup sugar
1 teaspoon vanilla extract
  (optional)
9-inch graham cracker crust

In 1-cup glass measure, sprinkle unflavored gelatine over ¼ cup cold water; let stand 2 minutes. Microwave at HIGH (Full Power) 40 seconds. Stir thoroughly, then let stand 2 minutes or until gelatine is completely dissolved.

Meanwhile, in large bowl, with electric mixer, beat cream cheese, sugar and vanilla until thoroughly blended. Gradually beat in gelatine mixture and remaining ¾ cup water until smooth. Pour into prepared crust; chill until firm, at least 1½ hours. Garnish, if desired, with fresh or canned fruit.

Makes 1 cheesecake or 8 servings

CONVENTIONAL DIRECTIONS: In small saucepan, sprinkle unflavored gelatine over ¼ cup cold water; let stand 1 minute. Stir over low heat until gelatine is completely dissolved, about 2 minutes. Proceed as above.

TRY THESE DELICIOUS VARIATIONS

Marbled Cheesecake: Before chilling, swirl in ⅓ cup chocolate fudge, butterscotch or your favorite flavor ice cream topping.

Lemon or Almond Cheesecake: Substitute ½ to ¾ teaspoon lemon or almond extract for vanilla extract.

Fruit 'n Creamy Cheesecake: Prepare cheesecake as above. Chill 10 minutes, then swirl in ⅓ cup strawberry or raspberry preserves.

Sunshine Cheesecake: Substitute ½ teaspoon orange extract for vanilla extract and add 1 teaspoon grated orange peel.

Chocolate Cheesecake: While beating, add ¼ cup unsweetened cocoa powder and ¼ cup additional sugar.

Pineapple Cheesecake: Substitute 1 cup canned pineapple juice for water.

Softening Cheeses
In microwave-safe bowl, place 1 package (8 ounces) unwrapped cream cheese and microwave at MEDIUM (50% Power) 1 minute or until softened. To bring ½ pound hard cheese, such as provolone, to room temperature, microwave unwrapped at MEDIUM 1 minute.

◆◆◆

BEVERAGES

FRUIT 'N SPICE MARGARITA

1 cup cold water
3 bags Lipton Special Blends
    Regular or Decaffeinated
    Orange & Spice Tea Bags
⅓ cup sugar

1 cup frozen strawberries
1½ tablespoons lemon juice
¼ cup tequila (optional)
1 cup ice cubes (about 6 to 8)

In 1-cup glass measure, combine water with orange & spice tea bags. Microwave at HIGH (Full Power) 2 minutes or until very hot. (Tea should not boil.) Let stand 5 minutes. Remove tea bags; stir in sugar and chill.

In blender, process tea, strawberries, lemon juice and tequila until blended. Add ice cubes, one at a time, and process at high speed until blended.

Makes about 2 servings

Variation: Use 3 Lipton Special Blends Raspberry or Blackberry Tea Bags.

CONVENTIONAL DIRECTIONS: Substitute 1 cup boiling water for cold water. In teapot, pour boiling water over orange & spice tea bags; cover and brew 5 minutes. Remove tea bags. Stir in sugar and chill. Proceed as above.

Fresh Fruit Juice
To get the most juice from a lemon, lime or orange, microwave at HIGH (Full Power) 30 seconds before squeezing.

◆◆◆

From left to right: Pink Tea Rose,
Lipton Iced Tea (see page 90)
and Fruit 'n Spice Margarita

PINK TEA ROSE

1 cup cold water
3 Lipton Flo-Thru Tea Bags
1 container (8 ounces) vanilla
   yogurt

1½ cups frozen strawberries
¼ cup cream of coconut

In 1-cup glass measure, combine water with tea bags. Microwave at HIGH (Full Power) 2 minutes or until very hot. (Tea should not boil.) Let stand 5 minutes. Remove tea bags; chill.

In blender, combine tea with remaining ingredients; process at high speed until blended. Garnish, if desired, with fresh strawberries.

Makes about 4 servings

CONVENTIONAL DIRECTIONS: Substitute 1 cup boiling water for cold water. In teapot, pour boiling water over tea bags; cover and brew 5 minutes. Remove tea bags. Proceed as above.

MAKE IT IN THE MICROWAVE

ONE SERVING AT A TIME . . .

Hot tea: Place 1 Lipton (cup-size) Flo-Thru Tea Bag in a 6-ounce microwave-safe cup, then fill with cold water. Microwave at HIGH (Full Power) 1½ to 2 minutes. (Tea should not boil.) Let stand ½ minute or to desired strength. Remove tea bag; squeeze.

Iced Tea: Place 1 Lipton (cup-size) Flo-Thru Tea Bag in a 12-ounce glass; pour ½ cup cold water over bag. Microwave at HIGH (Full Power) 1 minute.* (Tea should not boil.) Let stand ½ minute or to desired strength. Remove tea bag; squeeze. Fill glass with ice.

*Glass may be hot; use caution when removing from microwave oven.

. . . OR BY THE PITCHER

Iced Tea Pitcher: Place 2 Lipton Family Size Flo-Thru Tea Bags or 6 Regular (cup-size) Flo-Thru Tea Bags in a 2-cup microwave-safe measure, then fill with 1½ cups cold water. Microwave at HIGH (Full Power) 2 to 3 minutes. (Tea should not boil.) Let stand to desired strength: ½ minute for mild flavor; 3 minutes for full flavor. (Allow decaffeinated tea to stand 1 minute longer.) Remove tea bags; squeeze. Pour 4½ cups cold water into a large pitcher; stir in tea.

APPLE BERRY QUENCHER

2 cups apple juice	2 teaspoons lemon juice
8 Lipton Country Cranberry Herbal Tea Bags	1 cup chilled unsweetened white grape juice
2 tablespoons sugar	1 cup chilled club soda

In 2-cup glass measure, combine apple juice with country cranberry herbal tea bags. Microwave at HIGH (Full Power) 4½ minutes or until very hot. (Mixture should not boil.) Let stand 5 minutes. Remove tea bags; stir in sugar and cool.

In pitcher, combine tea, lemon and grape juice. Just before serving, add soda. Serve in ice-filled glasses and garnish, if desired, with lemon and apple slices.

Makes about 4 servings

CONVENTIONAL DIRECTIONS: Heat 2 cups apple juice to boiling. In teapot, pour hot apple juice over country cranberry herbal tea bags. Cover and brew 5 minutes. Remove tea bags; stir in sugar and cool. In pitcher, combine as above.

Apple Berry Wine Cooler: Substitute 1 cup dry white wine for grape juice.

FRESH MINT TEA JULEP

2 cups cold water	½ cup ice cubes (about 3 to 4)
6 Lipton Flo-Thru Tea Bags	1 cup chilled orange juice
⅓ cup sugar	½ cup fresh mint leaves

In 4-cup glass measure, combine cold water with tea bags. Microwave at HIGH (Full Power) 4 minutes or until very hot. (Tea should not boil.) Let stand 5 minutes. Remove tea bags. Stir in sugar until dissolved. Stir in ice cubes until melted to make 2½ cups liquid. In blender, combine tea with remaining ingredients; process at high speed until well blended. Strain over ice and garnish, if desired, with mint sprigs.

Makes about 4 servings

CONVENTIONAL DIRECTIONS: Substitute 2 cups boiling water for cold water. In teapot, pour boiling water over tea bags; cover and brew 5 minutes. Remove tea bags. Stir in sugar. In blender, combine tea with remaining ingredients; process at high speed until well blended. Serve as above.

Is it safe to put the tea bag in the microwave without removing the staples? It is not necessary to remove the staples from Lipton Tea Bags before microwaving. There is not sufficient metal to create arcing. Follow your microwave instructions and keep any metal away from the metal sides of the oven.

Why do the microwave instructions for tea say, "Do not boil"? Boiling the water in the microwave with the tea bag will give the tea a bitter flavor and may even produce a cloudy brew. To enjoy the "brisk" tea flavor of Lipton, never boil the tea bag.

◆◆◆

FIRESIDE PUNCH

1½ cups cranberry juice cocktail
1½ cups cold water
4 bags Lipton Cinnamon Apple
   or Gentle Orange Herbal
   Flo-Thru Tea Bags

2 tablespoons brown sugar
Cinnamon sticks (optional)
Fresh cranberries (optional)

In 1-quart glass measure or casserole, combine cranberry juice, water and cinnamon apple herbal tea bags. Microwave at HIGH (Full Power) 6 minutes or until very hot. (Mixture should not boil.) Let stand 5 minutes. Remove tea bags; stir in sugar. Pour into mugs and garnish with cinnamon sticks and fresh cranberries. *Makes about 5 servings*

CONVENTIONAL DIRECTIONS: In medium saucepan, bring cranberry juice and water to a boil. Add cinnamon apple herbal tea bags; cover and brew 5 minutes. Remove tea bags; stir in sugar. Serve as above.

APPLE & SPICE GROG

2 cups cold water
2 cups apple juice or cider
6 bags Lipton Regular or
   Decaffeinated Flo-Thru Tea
   Bags

1 cinnamon stick
3 whole cloves
3 tablespoons brown sugar
3 tablespoons rum or brandy
   (optional)

In 1½-quart glass measure or casserole, combine water, apple juice, tea bags, cinnamon and cloves. Microwave at HIGH (Full Power) 7 minutes or until very hot. (Mixture should not boil.) Let stand 5 minutes. Remove tea bags and spices; stir in sugar and rum. Serve in cups or mugs and garnish, if desired, with apple wedges. *Makes about 10 servings*

CONVENTIONAL DIRECTIONS: In large saucepan, combine water, apple juice, cinnamon and cloves; bring to a boil. Add tea bags; cover and brew 5 minutes. Remove tea bags and spices; stir in sugar and rum. Serve as above.

TEA TWISTER

1 cup cold water
2 Lipton Regular or
   Decaffeinated Flo-Thru Tea
   Bags

1 cup chilled grapefruit juice
1 cup chilled cranberry juice
   cocktail
2 tablespoons sugar

In 2-cup glass measure, combine water with tea bags. Microwave at HIGH (Full Power) 1½ minutes or until very hot. (Tea should not boil.) Let stand 5 minutes. Remove tea bags. Combine tea with remaining ingredients. Serve in ice-filled glasses and garnish, if desired, with wooden skewers threaded with fresh cranberries. *Makes about 2 servings*

CONVENTIONAL DIRECTIONS: Substitute 1 cup boiling water for cold water. In teapot, pour boiling water over tea bags; cover and brew 5 minutes. Remove tea bags. Combine remaining ingredients as above.

Fireside Punch

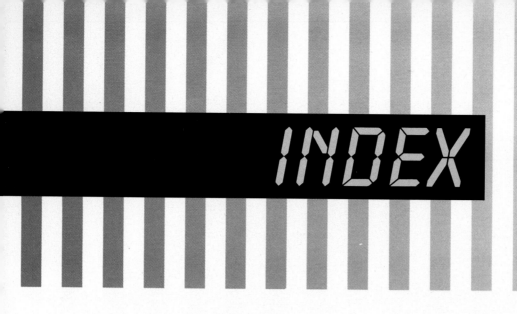

INDEX